A TIMELESS JOURNEY

LUC NIEBERGALL

Copyright © 2014 by Luc Niebergall

All rights reserved. This book or any portion thereof may not be reproduced or used in any manner whatsoever without the express written permission of the publisher except for the use of brief quotations in a book review.

Printed in the United States of America

First Edition, 2014

ISBN-10: 1501032836
ISBN-13: 978-1501032837

Kingdom Revelation Publishing

Table of Contents

Introduction 5

An Unexpected Meeting 9

The Detour 17

The Wisdom Of A Mystic 33

The Great Summoning 39

From Peasants To Royalty 51

Secrets Unfold 61

A Love That Is Wild 67

Falling Into Understanding 73

From Deep To Deep 85

The Creator's Heart 91

Renaissance Restored 101

Illuminated By Wisdom 107

Heaven's Many Courts 113

Knowledge, Wisdom and Revelation 121

Mantling Generations 135

Staying The Course 143

Equipped With Forgotten Tools 149

Journeying Through An Endless Ocean 157

Introduction

At the age of 16 I began an incredible journey into the bliss of the person, Jesus. When this journey began, a grace was released over my life to experience the living God through prophetic encounters. After eight years of visions, dreams and heavenly encounters, I felt like the Lord spoke to me and told me to write a book in story form about some of the things that I had experienced. To the best of my ability I have tried to record everything exactly the way that I saw and heard it. However, there are some places in this book where my memory was hazy, so I therefore took the liberty to fill in the gaps as I felt led by Holy Spirit. There are also some places where I have expanded upon for the purpose of writing flow; as this book is not intended to be a compilation of stories but a single narrative. Much of my time, laughter and tears have been put into this book. In many ways, by writing and publishing it, I am inviting you into my personal journey with Christ.

I by no means expect you to take what is written in this book as the definitive word of the Lord. This is not Scripture. Period. However, I do encourage you to have an openness to what the Lord may speak to you through it. Where some of the revelations in this book are more specifically applicable to my personal life, most are truths that can be applied on a broader scale. Some of what I have written may strike you as being outside of the realm of possibility. However, some things with God are 100% relational and emotional, so they cannot be caught intellectually, only experientially. Since this is the case, feel free to put yourself in my shoes as you read. While writing I have made the main character (myself) gender neutral for this very purpose. Allow yourself to experience that which I have had the privilege to experience.

Life is supposed to be a wonderful and worshipful adventure that continually leads us deeper into the heart of our Creator. As we grow in Him, we are refined as His sons and daughters. We are revealed as kings and queens. My hope through this book is that confidence and assurance will be solidified in your identity. Sons and daughters of God, kings and queens of the kingdom of heaven, take your stand in confidence because your Father in heaven is delighted in who you are.

Introduction

I bless you to know your identity. I bless you to know who were created to be. You are important and irreplaceable in God's heart. You are an eternal well of greatness waiting to be discovered.

An Unexpected Meeting

itting upon the sandy shore of Heaven, I looked over the roaring sea into the eyes of the most beautiful sunrise I have ever seen. The sun spilled forth in vibrant whites, yellows and reds that were woven together masterfully. Full clouds stood before the rise, as a red carpet set in place to present the sun's arrival. However, the light reflecting off of the clouds was not red. It was an array of colours that I have never seen in all of my years. They were Heaven's colours.

As my eyes beheld the sunrise, gentle snowflakes descended to kiss my face. I found myself perplexed by the harmony of the weather. The weather somehow lived in a perfect balance of spring, summer, autumn and winter all at the same time. The sense of expectancy that accompanied spring existed hand-in-hand with autumn's kind grace. The language of summer partnered with winter's pure voice. Each season held matched authority, existing fully to compliment its counterpart, creating a perfect ensemble of comfort.

Heaven's wind blew, whispering sonnets that could not have been composed by the greatest of song writers. The great wind was so dense that it did not time its path around my form. It would instead wrap itself around me like a fabric before it would continue its journey throughout the morning skies.

The sun continued to rise from behind the distant ocean line, inviting my hope to rise with it. *Could beauty have chosen a more exquisite form to present itself?* I thought.

Soaking in bliss, I closed my eyes turning inwards to the peace that was beginning to birth inside of me. As I delved deep into myself, I found assurance. I found joy. A warm breeze embraced me. It held me. Nurtured me. The heat of the sun started a fire within. It was no ordinary fire. It was a fire that burned away any preconceived thoughts of who I was and left someone who was secure and confident in its wake. In that moment I was whole.

I do not know how long I sat in this moment for. However, I could have basked in it for a lifetime, and it would have been a life well lived. This place was life. This place was home.

As I rested in the moment, a sudden sound arose. It was the sound of an instrument. A flute in fact. I listened as the simple melodic song harmonized with the wind.

Opening my eyes, I looked in the direction from which the song came to see someone sitting next to me. How this person appeared without my detection, I have not the slightest of clue. The person appeared to be a man in his late fifties. However, the angelic glow that shone from his face revealed to me that he was no mere man. With his head tilted towards the sunrise, he played his gentle song. Creation seemed to respond. The trees would hypnotically sway to the song's rhythm. His dignified posture and apparel presented him as scholarly. Hiding behind modest robes, I could tell that he was one who undeniably held profound integrity and insight.

"What is your name?" I whispered. I would have spoken louder, but the sunrise's beauty still held my breath captive.

Pulling the flute away from his mouth, he let his eyes humbly fall to the distant waves. "I have many names, my friend. I have names that only the trees and mountains can pronounce. I also have names that only the birds of the air and the fish of the sea can speak. My reputation has echoed throughout history, yet my words purpose to glorify One whose name is not my own." He lingered in silence, then continued, "I am the chief messenger of the King of kings. Those who dwell on Earth call me Gabriel."

Gabriel turned the question around. Yet instead of simply asking me what my name was, he asked a more profound question. "Tell me friend, who are you?"

I looked away, suddenly feeling unsure of myself. Just a moment ago, I felt like I knew who I was for the first time in my entire life. No insecurity blinded me from seeing who I was created to be. Confidence was my reality instead of a fantasy that felt out of hand's grasp. The sun gave me all the clarity I needed. But now, for whatever reason, I felt as though my identity had been veiled once again. The truth was that I did not know who I was. *Will I ever understand who I was created to be? Or will I forever be nameless and faceless?*

Purposeless.

Alone.

My eyes ascended back to the sun in hope that its light would brighten my understanding once again.

Nothing came. My identity was silent.

Realization struck me that I had not said anything for a few minutes. How could I respond to a question that was as complex as it was simple? Even though this was the first time I had met this fascinating angel, he called me friend, and for whatever reason it felt right. I could trust him. Deciding that honesty was the best road to take I said, "I am a servant of the most high God. However, I do not know my name. I do not know who I am."

A light, unexpected laugh came from Gabriel. "Well, you are not going to be of much use if you do not know who you are, will you?" He then said more seriously, "Those who do not yet know the Father believe they are orphans. Those who believe they are orphans will adopt the world as their mother. They will honour her words, and embrace her lies as their identity. The world tries to bury sons and daughters with orphanship. Soon enough you will meet the Father. He will give you your name."

Gabriel's words held great authority. Where his instrumental song sailed upon the breeze, his words cut right through the thickest of winds and penetrated into the deepest places of my heart. Something in me could not help but allow excitement to swell. The Father would name me...

He continued, "Until you receive your true name, for now, you will be known as Nameless One."

An Unexpected Meeting

Not being overly fond of my "new name", I shrugged off what felt like an insult and asked, "Gabriel, why have you come to me?" Momentum was returning to my speech.

"The King of kings often sends me with a message whenever history is about to take a new course of direction. For whatever reason, He has chosen for me to come to you. The message is this: the sons and daughters of the living God are about to discover their value. Every nation will gather. Governments, kings and queens will stand in awe. All will rally around the sight of a Father lavishing love upon His children. This is the key that will unlock the Kingdom of Heaven to conquer every stream of society. This is the era of the sons and daughters of the living God."

As Gabriel prophesied about the great revival of identity that would take place, the ocean responded with a roar. The mightiest waves I have ever seen ascended to as high as seventy feet. They crashed and rolled over one another in worship. A groan shouted out from underneath the sand, deep from the bowels of Heaven. All of creation rejoiced.

I could hear a sudden choir in the distance joining creation in its song. As Gabriel looked head on into the sunrise, I turned back to where the choir's song came. The beautiful song travelled over distant mountains and through vast forests to meet me on the luminous shore. Based upon the volume and fullness of the sound, I guessed that there must have been millions of vocalists, if not billions. Whoever was singing, their song of victory shook all of Heaven. Gabriel sang along with them:

*"The softest tear from the Father's heart,
mightily holds the night at bay.
The smallest laugh from a child now brought,*

A smiling Son to call forth the day."

*"Laying still the broken sleep,
awaiting those who wield the light.
The living sword will pierce the deep,
the healing streams will free their strife."*

"Where is that song coming from?" I asked Gabriel.

"There is an important meeting taking place in the Centre Assembly of Heaven. This is where the great choir is worshipping the one true God." Gabriel then said, "Every living saint whose heart is for the Kingdom of Heaven's advancement will be at this meeting. Many saints who have already ascended into eternity will also be there."

I was about to ask if I was also to be at this meeting, when a sudden coolness covered the shore on which I sat. I looked towards the sun, which was now blotted out by a great bird who quickly descended in the direction of Gabriel and I. The choir resounded once again in a song of praise and declaration:

*"Creation shouts with forceful groans,
calling forth the kings and queens.
To marry all of Earth's abode,
with Heaven's fast-reviving seed."*

Within seconds the great bird was sitting beside me, opposite to Gabriel. It was an eagle. Not just any eagle; it was an enormous eagle. If I were standing, it would have still towered over me by at least a foot. The eagle was pure white, other than the royal gold on the very tip of each feather. My breath was instantly stolen once again by the sight of him.

An Unexpected Meeting

Motioning to the daunting bird, Gabriel said, "This is Journey. He is here to carry you to the great meeting."

I looked into Journey's big eyes. They were eyes that told innumerable stories. The bright green and orange spheres did not just look at me, they looked into me. My heart pounded. I could feel a part of me that was dead and forgotten beginning to breathe. Any dust that covered this aspect of my identity was blown away by winds of grace. Resurrection was occurring within me. I could feel an unfamiliar emotion beginning to take shape. Was it passion? No. It was something new. It was a hunger for adventure. It was a thirst to go where only this eagle could take me.

I ripped my eyes from the bird, to look back at Gabriel, who held a steady smile on his face. I knew in my heart that I was about to begin a journey that would change the very essence of who I was forever. In that moment, the part of me that craved comfort and complacency was silent for the first time that I can remember. I smiled back at Gabriel. Allowing excitement to push words past any barriers of timidity, I said to him, "I want to leave immediately."

The Detour

n Journey's back, I sailed upon thick waves of wind. With my fingers clenched onto his golden feathers, I took notice of how Journey never missed a current. He was a master of flight. I felt a strange oneness with the bird that I cannot explain. When I first met Journey and looked into his eyes, it felt as though the eagle instantly became more than an acquaintance to me; more than a friend. Journey became a part of who I was. I often would not even need to speak aloud because he seemed attuned to my very thoughts. When the bird would catch a gust, or take a new course of direction, it seemed as though I would often know what he was going to do before even doing it.

Seeing Heaven from a bird's eye view was overwhelming to say the least. We travelled away from the shore's oceanic view and over vast forests, towards Heaven's colossal mountains. However, these mountains were by no means ordinary. Each mountain looked as though it was an enormous gem stone set into the ground of Heaven. I could see an entire mountain made of onyx, another made completely of sapphire and another of diamond. There were mountains of emerald, amethyst and jasper. Each glowed brilliantly, reflecting morning's light. The different streams throughout Heaven were mesmerizing. The water was so clear that I could actually see right to the bottom of each river even from the hight we were flying.

The choir that I heard back on Heaven's shore grew louder, still forcefully advancing over the mountains as we flew throughout the skies of Heaven.

We were not the only ones who soared throughout the expansive air. Numerous birds that were about five feet tall darted through the skies. These birds were clothed in flames, yet their skin or feathers were never marred. They were phoenixes. I watched truly marveling. The legendary birds bolted from one end of the sky to the other like shooting stars. They were there one second and gone the next.

As I watched the ancient birds, something big caught my eye that flew in the far distance. It must have been at least 20 times the size of Journey. However, it was no bird. It was a dragon. The fabled creature was right before my eyes. I was astonished at the sight of it. Normally anything that size would startle me at first sight, but there was such an atmosphere of peace, joy and love in Heaven that I knew nothing evil or harmful could ever exist in this glorious place. It was truly a creature of grace. Paying no attention to us, the dragon elegantly swept through the sky, as its long tail brushed the breeze with masterful strokes. Its scales resembled diamonds, glimmering in purity. I had never seen a creature that carried such a well-rounded balance of power and grace all at once.

On the ground I could see snow-white lions running in packs through emerald-green plains. Their quick and powerful strides were hardly comprehendible to me. Beside them ran a herd of sheep. They trotted fearlessly beside the lions in peace, seeming as though they were in pure fellowship with the mighty beasts. Heaven was such a wondrous place. Even though I knew

The Detour

that I would experience it for eternity, I was certain that I would always be fascinated and surprised by how dramatically whimsical it was. It felt like I was living a dream. Yet my heart told me that it was more. This was reality. It was truth.

I sensed that Journey was about to take a detour instead of immediately going to the meeting. Before giving thought to whether the eagle could even speak, a question slipped out from my mouth. "Where are we going, Journey?" After I asked the question, I waited for a response, unsure as to whether one would come at all.

Journey then spoke in a calm voice. It was a voice that was strong, yet was not hard or uninviting in any way. "Nameless One, before we go to the meeting I am taking you to the Waterfall of Understanding that flows from the onyx mountain. It is of utmost importance that you drink from its River of Revelation before attending the meeting."

That one answer from Journey filled my mind with more questions than I even knew what to do with. What was a Waterfall of Understanding? Or a River of Revelation? Why did I need to go there before attending the meeting? However, I knew that all of those questions could wait, because when I heard Journey call me 'Nameless One', one question stood out more than any other.

I asked him hesitantly, "Journey, do you know my real name?"

I could feel the great eagle's compassion begin to swell for me. "I know your real name, Nameless One. I have known it since the foundations of the Earth were made. Even though I hold great influence and favour with you, you would not believe me even if I told you. True names can only be received through an encounter with the Father. True sons and daughters always find their identity in the Father. They refuse to find it in anywhere else."

Currents of wind rolled over my cheeks softly. "And do you know the Father? Will you bring me to Him?" I asked.

"Yes, I know Him. He and I are very good friends, you know. I will take you to Him in due time. However, for now there are more immediate truths for you to learn."

As we drifted throughout vast skies, even amongst my current surroundings my focus delved inwards. My thoughts dwelled with my desire to meet the Father. Longing and aspiration held me there for the rest of our flight to the onyx mountain.

Nearing closer to the mountain, I began to hear the waterfall thundering against the colossus onyx gem stone. In that moment, I looked upon a mountain that I am sure stood taller than all of the mountains on Earth combined. My mind could not even comprehend its height. Not only was it gigantic, but all of the money on Earth would not have even come close to equaling in price what this onyx gem would have been worth. Journey ascended higher and higher, close to the top of the mountain where the waterfall resided.

We finally landed on a sizable ledge. I looked over Journey's body to see the shimmering mountain beneath us. Climbing off his back, I placed my feet on the priceless stone and looked down again at the black-onyx floor. I could see my own reflection. Heaven was full of abundant riches indeed.

The Detour

Thundering before me was the Waterfall of Understanding. Up to that point I had never known that water this pure existed. A pale, yet endearing blue passionately rushed out from clefts of black stone. Streams of gold and silver were entwined throughout the water's fall. The water from the waterfall fell into a pool, which quickly converted into a river. Looking down the mountain, I could see that the river flowed all the way to the mountain's bottom, and throughout different places in Heaven.

Looking over at Journey, I could see that he already sensed every question that had entered my mind. He said to me, "This mountain is not simply a mountain that consists of onyx. Its primary purpose is not to impress the eyes; it is a place of great importance. This is the Mountain of Intercession. Most of the moves of God that you have studied throughout the course of history have taken place because of the battles that have been fought and won on this very mountain. Ever since we entered the Age of the End-Times, men and women have met on this mountain in prayer for the nations of Earth."

I knelt down right in front of the river that flowed from the waterfall and touched its silky water. My fingers began to tingle. There was a depth to this water. Looking into it was like looking into a well of wisdom. For a time, I sat there, gazing in wonderment at how even the simplest of things in Heaven were undeniably great.

Then something peculiar began to happen. The water began portraying shapes and pictures. It was as though I was watching a screen that projected images. In the water, I began seeing visions of past movements of prayer throughout history. I saw visions of the prayer movement that took place with the desert fathers in 300AD. Not only did I see the saints praying, but I also saw how different nations were directly impacted through their intercession. I saw visions of men and women praying in Ireland in 558AD, in the 300 year prayer movement. I then saw people from present times praying for a revival that would sweep across the entire world. On the watery screen I saw the prayers of the saints pull on the Heavens so that it could make Earth its dwelling place. I saw how prayer would be a pivotal catalyst to entire cities knowing the love of God. I spoke out loud to myself quietly, "How have we overlooked such a powerful and essential part of co-laboring with God?"

Slowly looking back up to Journey, I saw him nod his head, motioning in instruction for me to take a drink. With slight wavering, my hand dipped in, cupping a handful of shimmering water. I lifted my hand to my mouth and took a drink. Liquid from the River of Revelation danced down my throat. I waited, expecting something unexpected to happen. Yet nothing did. I looked up to Journey confused. Not feeling the slightest change, I stood up to walk back to him, when I suddenly fell face forward right onto the black stone. I laid prostrate, completely intoxicated by the water's purity. I was so intoxicated to the point where it felt impossible to even think or see straight.

I slowly flipped onto my back, when my memory called forth a verse that I had previously heard from the choir's song:

> *"Creation shouts with forceful groans,*
> *calling forth the kings and queens.*
> *To marry all of Earth's abode,*
> *with Heaven's fast-reviving seed."*

The poem rang throughout my spirit, calling forth a compassion for the broken hearted that was unfathomable. To say that I wept would be a drastic understatement. Yet, at the same time, what I did was

The Detour

very different than weeping entirely considering that sadness nor tears existed in this place. The response elicited in me was far more profound than weeping. I was taking on the very heart of God for His children. A desire to see this beautiful culture I was experiencing in Heaven, becoming every person's individual experience on the Earth overtook me. Obsession for the love of the one true God to touch every human being was transforming me. I can honestly say that I had never felt such a profound love for people in all my life, up until that point.

    I started praying for different individuals. I prayed for prostitutes, business men, orphans and all sorts of leaders in the world. I interceded for the widows and the broken hearted. I then began praying for the salvation, healing and deliverance of entire cities and nations. I prayed that a hunger for revival would ignite in the heart of the church to such anextent that the entire world would be transformed into the likeness of Heaven. Laying prostrate, I interceded endlessly. The thought to stop praying did not even cross my mind once. Ceasing was not only something I could not comprehend in that moment, the option simply did not exist to me. It could not exist because I felt as though I stepped outside of time entirely. So, I did only what I could do. I prayed and believed for a move of God that would turn the world right-side-up.

Journey's Counsel

pon the onyx floor I laid, lost in encounters with the Lord and consumed in unrelenting prayer. The stone pressed cold against my face, yet my external awareness was greatly muted by my internal experiences with the heart of God. Much time passed when I suddenly heard what sounded like a distant voice calling to me:

"Nameless One! Nameless One!"

The voice sounded like Journey's. I was so lost and consumed in what I was doing that his strong tone, instead of drawing my attention, just agitated me.

"Nameless One! It is time; we must leave now."

Even though Journey's voice was sound, it seemed highly muffled considering how concentrated I was. As faint as his utterances were, his dull voice did not escape my awareness. Yet considering the profoundness of my experience, to stop praying did not feel like a practical option. My compassion and hunger forced me to dismiss his voice as only a distant sound. It did not matter to me. I needed to continue praying.

It seemed as though much time had passed since the distant voice disturbed me, possibly hours, when suddenly a massive talon grabbed my shoulder and jerked me. "Nameless One, it is time for you to stop."

I looked over to see that it was Journey.

Journey's appearance looked far more detailed to me in comparison to before I began interceding. The intricacies of his being were now discernible to my eyes. It was not that he had changed. It was something about me that had changed. My eyes somehow seemed clearer. My perception of Heaven was more refined. "Journey, why is it that I can see more clearly now?"

Journey responded, "Each mountain in Heaven holds a Waterfall of Understanding. Yet, the Rivers of Revelation from each waterfall impart different truths to those who drink. When you drank from the river, you received understanding of God's heart for Heaven to invade Earth. You have been interceding for this to occur for much longer than you would think, Nameless One. As you prayed, you were taking on the heart of God. As you took on His heart, your own began to harmonize with His. Therefore your faith and understanding of Heaven has heightened, which has refined your perception. This is why your consciousness of Heaven is now clearer."

Journey went on to say, "It was of utmost importance that we came here before attending the meeting. It was essential that you encountered the heart of God for His children before stepping into greater realms of revelation and understanding. It would have been nearly impossible for you to understand what it looked like to believe for Heaven to invade Earth if your perception of Heaven was unclear."

I looked down to the onyx floor once again seeing my reflection. I looked older. I could see fresh wisdom set in my demeanor.

"Journey, you said that I was praying for longer than I would think. How long have I been praying?"

Without even knowing it, my question for Journey began to unravel a teaching that I did not expect would come. Journey let silence fill the air before he responded:

"Before I answer that question, you must understand that time in Heaven is different than time on Earth. One second in Heaven can be the same as one thousand years on Earth. One thousand years in Heaven can be the same as one second on Earth. This means that one circumstance in Heaven that lasted one second, could take 10 years to unfold on Earth; and vice-versa. That being said, what only felt like a few hours to you here, was really an entire season of prayer that you had lived out on Earth, which lasted five years. Where with your body you were on Earth praying and encountering the Lord, with your spirit you were here on this mountain."

I sunk back in near disbelief at what Journey told me. I could not even begin to wrap my head around how Heaven and Earth were woven together in such a way. I could remember the season that Journey spoke of. I remembered the time when I first became consumed with the presence of the Lord. With all of my time I obsessively sought Him for five years straight, while focusing much of my efforts in intercession for a move of God on Earth.

Looking at Journey in sheer shock, he calmed me by saying, "I know, I know. This is usually the reaction people have when they have seen Heaven and have experienced how its time can ebb and flow. It was a rather good season you had though. Much was accomplished not only for yourself, but for many through your intercession. It was important for you to come here to encounter the heart of God to such a great extent before attending the meeting."

"You mean to say that the meeting is still taking place after all this time?"

"Of course. Meetings like this take time you know," Journey said with a hint of amusement in his tone.

Journey then continued, almost sounding faintly reluctant in his speech. "There is something that you should know, Nameless One; although you may not enjoy hearing what I have to say. I will give you the choice as to whether you would like to listen. If you choose not to hear then you will be granted comfort, because you will be pillowed by ignorance. However, if you choose to hear my words then you will learn a lesson of great importance even though it may bring you discomfort at first."

I would be lying if I said that I did not hesitate. Yet, even though I craved comfort, I knew that I needed to hear what Journey had to say. "Tell me, Journey."

"Wise choice, Nameless One. I called you earlier to stop your season of intercession, but you disobeyed my call and continued to pray. Do you remember this?"

I thought back calling forth the memory. As it caught up with me I nodded my head, waiting for Journey to continue.

"You did not realize it at the time, but the time between you disobeying my call, and me stopping your intercession just now may have only felt like a few hours here in Heaven, however, on Earth it was in fact one year and three months. Your compassion forced you into seeing more urgency in the need, than having an urgency in obeying the word of the Lord for your life. I allowed you to pray for another year and three months; however, now we are behind schedule in what you need to learn by that same amount of time."

Journey's words hit me like a ton of bricks. How could one small mistake derail me so profoundly? "Why did you not force me to stop, Journey? I did not understand that there would be so much consequence behind that one small choice," I said in a form of shock.

"I did not force you to stop because you have free will to do as you please."

Clearly reading the frustration with myself on my face, Journey began to expand upon what had happened. As he did, he never let gentleness escape his tone. "Consider this a lesson, Nameless One. Every good leader must be risen up in the secret place with God, learning to take on His heart for His children, which you have just done. However, you should have listened when I first called you. Now we are behind schedule because you did not discern properly the urgency of my call. You were doing the right thing, but in the wrong season. Many saints end up years behind in their ministries because they fail to do the right thing in the right season. It is important to understand the times and seasons for your life, otherwise you remain as a reed flapping in the wind aimlessly. Within every season is a correct posture to position yourself. If you hold an improper posture then you can risk prolonging your season. You need to learn to lie down in green pastures, to be led by still waters, and to walk through valleys."

I looked back down at my reflection, eyes still wide, hardly able to comprehend that I was on this mountain for five years praying. Hardly able to come to terms with the fact that my one mistake of dismissing Journey's voice had put me behind schedule one year and three months in what I needed to learn. Yet, although Journey was correcting me, I could not help but feel fed while sitting under his counsel. Listening to him project revelation was like soaking in words of gold that were refining my very being. What a lesson to be learned, I thought.

"It is important for you to understand, Nameless One, that those who are willing to receive discipline from the Lord, which you just did, are granted access to greater doors of revelation. You receive access to doors that others do not get to walk through simply because you have allowed yourself to be chastened. Now, since you have willingly swallowed the difficult truth, you can be trusted with another that should greatly encourage you."

Hope sparked inside of me.

"With a heart willing to learn from this lesson, God will in due time restore whatever time has been lost. It is not considered wise to stumble in the same way over and over again. If you refuse to learn and continue to stumble, there will be great consequences because of your disobedience. Know that it would not be the Lord willing such consequences, considering that you do not live in the Era of Judgement. Instead, you would be willing these consequences upon yourself by not renewing your mind by the revelation you are now receiving. Those who are truly repentant learn from their mistakes and move on to greater glories. This, God will reward by restoring what has been lost, for your steps are ordained by Him. So do not fret, Nameless one. Be encouraged and simply change the way you think."

Waves of relief swept over me.

Journey's Counsel

"Even though we have already spent far too much time on this mount, there is one last message that needs to be deposited into your spirit before we leave," Journey declared.

With my head held high I listened as wind wove around the mountain's body, caressing its form. Before I even had the opportunity to meditate on everything that had just occurred, I suddenly began to feel my skin tingle in a rather odd way. It was as though I could feel dew from Heaven gently resting upon me. With my eyes still raised, I saw that a cloud was beginning to materialize to envelope the section of mountain where Journey and I were meeting. Where before daylight had shone vibrantly it was now paled by a cloudy fog.

As the cloud wrapped around me, creating an atmosphere of cool dampness, it suddenly felt hard to stand again. I slouched to the ground sitting cross legged, as I could feel my heart beginning to yoke with the heart of God once again. Delight rushed through my soul. I was thrilled to be in touch with His overwhelming heart. It felt as though I was being clothed in heavenly glory. Chills ran up and down me as the cloud of glory dwelled among us.

Lost in a shroud of emotion yet again, I saw that about 20 paces behind Journey, a shape began emerging through the cloud. In seconds the shape pushed through the foggy air into plain sight, revealing a man. This man looked both human and divine. I somehow knew that this was not an angel like Gabriel. It was a man who had already ascended to Heaven and was now in his heavenly form. The contrast between his humanness and heavenliness was sobering. This man was shorter in height and wore a simple robe; yet, light radiated from him from head to toe. As strips of lightening shot from his body, I could not help but be moved by the sense of purity that accompanied him. Even though his face shone brightly, his facial features were simple, looking like a man's face should.

Journey glanced over to me and said, "This is a great man of God, who in his lifetime in the 1600's restored a revelation to the global church concerning intimacy with the Lord. While you were praying, I called for him to come and meet with you because there is an important message that I have asked him to share with you."

Even though Journey did not mention his name, I knew exactly who this man was. Standing before me was Brother Lawrence, the Christian monk who pioneered a revelation of the presence of God.

The Wisdom Of A Mystic

umility emitted from Brother Lawrence. Being in his presence, I knew that I had never been in the company of a person who walked so closely with God.

Brother Lawrence approached me and took a seat upon the stony floor. Across from me, he sat cross legged. I now sat upon the onyx mountain, face to face with one of the most well-known mystics in Christendom. Neither of us took the initiative to officially introduce each other. It did not feel as though we needed to. It was as if we both knew each other already. Brother Lawrence took his time before he began to speak, showing that he was in no rush at all. He just sat for a time, basking in the atmosphere of glory. When he did finally speak, he spoke with a soft grace. His voice was delicate; as smooth as a flower's pedal. Yet, the words that travelled upon it were not delicate in the slightest. His words spun truths that were impenetrable and without cracks. He spoke with both love and authority:

"Every good leader must become lost in the heart of God. They must become lost in His presence," Brother Lawrence said. "What you just experienced when you drank water from the River of Revelation is what every ministry, or life for that matter, should be built upon. It should be built upon a non-stop intimate encounter with the heart of God. Many build their lives upon a philosophy, doctrine or principal. Yet, wisdom beckons us to build life upon a person, the Son of Man."

As Brother Lawrence spoke, the cloud still rested softly upon us. As it enshrouded us, I could see within the cloud what looked like intricate gold and silver flakes hovering throughout the clouded sky. As the cloud thickened in numerous areas, it took on a pearly white coloration. It created a mysterious atmosphere, yet it did not in any way feel negative. What was stirring in me in that moment was actually a hunger for mystery. A hunger to venture through the undiscovered aspects of God's heart. Sitting with Brother Lawrence, I could tell that this was the culture that he eternally experienced; an unbroken thirst for the things unknown. As he spoke, I could sense that he was inviting me to experience the same. A part of me wanted to speak; to ask questions. Yet, words would not escape my mouth because I felt so undone by the revelation of friendship with the Lord that was taking root deep inside of me. So instead of prodding him with questions, I just remained quiet and carried on in listening.

Brother Lawrence continued, "There is a question that God is asking the church in this day. This one question is the most important test that any believer will ever face. The question is this: Do you remember your first love? Many will allow circumstance to sway them from true friendship with God. Others will allow relationships to stand before their love for Him. Ministry and work have taken priority over intimacy with the Lord in many people's hearts. Yet, those who hold onto Him and choose to fall deeper in love with Him in each moment will receive the greatest reward indeed. Their reward will be the deep places of His heart. They will experience a love that is wild. A love that is untamable."

"It is this place of closeness that will bring true healing to the nations. It is one thing to minister because it feels like the right thing to do. It is another thing entirely to minister because you have been moved by an encounter with the love of God."

Even though the truths that Brother Lawrence spoke were simple, I knew that they would take years, if not, a lifetime to digest. I looked over at Journey, who stood at a distance, looking beyond the cliff into the thick fog of glory. I could tell that he was attentive to what Brother Lawrence was saying, yet I doubted that what he taught was anything new to Journey. Even though Journey was often quiet during our flight to the onyx mountain, as we spent more time together, great wisdom began to unfold from him. I knew that behind his strong beak was an endless fountain of revelation.

Suddenly in that moment, Journey did speak up. With his face still gazing into foggy skies he said, "Lawrence, why don't you share some revelation about spiritual warfare with him? I am sure he would benefit greatly from it."

"Ah yes," Brother Lawrence responded as though he was waiting for Journey to ask him to share on that particular subject. The way Journey talked to him made it seem as though they were familiar with one another. Perhaps even that they had already been acquainted for quite some time.

"Many have an unhealthy fear of spiritual warfare," Brother Lawrence said authoritatively. "Warfare is very real, but many have a tendency to overcomplicate it. Warfare is simple. The entire purpose of spiritual warfare is to try and sway sons and daughters from their identity. Once sons and daughters choose to believe a lie concerning who they are, the enemy has ground to attack. He has ground to attack because they have forgotten who they are and, therefore, forget to stand in the benefits of their birthright."

As Brother Lawrence explained this, my mind darted to different churches I knew of that were taken out entirely by spiritual attack. I thought of the many men and women of God who had mighty fallouts from ministry and marriage. It was true what Brother Lawrence said; all of these fallouts, whether for an individual or entire congregations, first started with identity that was compromised. It started with sons and daughters forgetting that they were sons and daughters. This led them to make choices as though they were fatherless. That was when a lie could be planted. Unfortunately, when those lies were not corrected, they developed into greater lies until chaos occurred.

"So, then what is the answer to warfare?" Brother Lawrence asked, interrupting my train of thought. "If warfare is simple then the solution must also be simple. The solution is simple because truth is simple. Many try to complicate truth by wrapping it up in intellectualism, but it really is elementary. Abide under the shelter and covering of God's wings. Abide in intimacy and friendship and you are untouchable to the enemy. Overcoming the enemy's tactics has nothing to do with battling; it has everything to do with abiding. It has everything to do with being. There are many world-wide leaders who have fallen. This is because when we forfeit intimacy with the Lord, we forfeit our protection. He is our shield; nothing else. Not our knowledge, reputation, relationships; nothing but Him."

"Many world-wide leaders have finished their race with excellence because they have chosen to remember their first love. They have chosen to be consumed by the love of God towards them, and have chosen to hold their love and friendship with Him above all things. When you truly choose Him, you will dwell with Him. Dwell in Him.

You will be unswayable in your identity, knowing that the enemy's power cowers before the love that the Father has towards you."

"God is raising up different individuals and ministries in the Earth to refocus the eyes of the church. Those who have been appointed this mandate will teach the Bride of Christ that she will only walk in an authority to rule and reign when she knows how to romance with the Son of Man. These messengers will come with a message of intimacy and friendship with the Lord, so that the church's eyes may never be taken off the One who pioneered freedom and authored life."

Brother Lawrence then looked deep into my eyes and declared, "The message that I am to give you is simple. Just Jesus. Truth is simple. Just Jesus. Life is simple. Just Jesus. Remember your first love."

On that note, Brother Lawrence stood up, showing me that the message that he came to share with me was now complete. I began quickly running everything he spoke to me through my head, so that I would not forget even a single word.

I looked over to Journey, who was still standing by the cliff's edge, looking as eager as ever to take flight. "Come, Nameless One, you have been summoned to the great meeting. If we do not leave now then we risk missing it." I slowly walked to Journey and climbed aboard his back. I looked back at the onyx mountain, again taken in by how the sun's light shimmered upon the dark stone. I looked upon the mystic, who still by the sight of him ignited a thirst within me for things unknown. Lastly I looked at the sparkling, rushing water that coursed throughout the Waterfall of Understanding. Longing filled me to take another drink. Desire urged me to be so attuned to the very feelings of God's heart once again.

A Timeless Journey

Before Journey and I took flight out of the cloud of glory and away from the onyx mountain, Brother Lawrence's eyes stole my attention for a final moment. He spoke forth a last revelation, as if to drive his message home to forever abide in my heart.

"Never leave this place of intimacy, Nameless One. Never leave this place of friendship with God. This is the key to a fruitful life. This is the key to true peace and joy. Everything that you ever do in your life that can be called great will always be the by-product of you remembering your first love. Venturing through the depths of the heart of God is not meant to be just an experience, or even a season; it is meant to be an eternal lifestyle."

The Great Summoning

Wind current by wind current, Journey and I travelled forth to the great meeting. The closer we got, the higher anticipation built within me. The nearer we were, the more that the air became electric and thick with substance. A swell of emotion reigned in the atmosphere.

It was only moments before the meeting place was in plain view, when my eyes were met by a wonderful sight.

The meeting place was a vast garden. This garden was the embodiment of perfection. From the most intricate blade of grass, to the largest boulder, every aspect of this garden was crafted flawlessly and purposefully set in place. This particular garden projected an aroma of intimacy; much like I experienced on the onyx mountain. I was beginning to understand that there were different anointings in different places throughout Heaven. You could tangibly feel it. There were different anointings in each place, because each destination carried a grace to impart a specific truth. When I was first told of the meeting place where the saints gathered, I had assumed it would be smaller in vicinity; however, this garden was so grand that it would have probably required weeks of constant travel to get from one end to the other. In Heaven, even though this garden was enormous, the entire scope of it was discernible to my eyes. It occurred to me that I probably would not have been able to see such distances if my perception of Heaven had not been heightened when my heart was yoked with God's.

The army of saints that filled the garden were more innumerable than the stars; and many shone as such. I could see many great angels; some who stood on the outskirts of the garden and others who were woven in throughout the crowd. At the very front of the great choir stood a tree that towered proudly well over 300 feet tall. Even from the very back entry of the garden I could see how the tree shone in golden splendor. It was clothed by a mane of leaves that were so diverse in appearance that not one single leaf could be compared to another.

Pointing, I directed, "Journey, look at that tree!"

Journey laughed aloud, "That is the Tree of Life. On it are the leaves that will bring healing to the nations. This meeting place is called the Garden of Intimacy."

Sobriety hit me immediately. This was the Garden of Intimacy. I knew in my spirit that the garden that Adam and Eve communed with God in on Earth, had to have been a reflection to this masterpiece.

Journey and I finally descended. After landing, I got to press my feet upon the garden's soft lawn for the first time. From that feeling I knew that I needed to take this opportunity to explore. Without taking the time to decide whether it was a good idea or not, I patted Journey's thick coat of feathers reassuring him that I would be back soon. Leaving him at the back of the army, I stepped further into the vast crowd of saints.

Curiosity took its lead.

⸺⸻

I wove throughout the fabric of saints. Never before had I seen so many people assembled in one place. The biggest of stadiums could not have contained such a group. Men, women and children from every tribe and nation filled the garden, basking in the presence of the Lord. I took notice that many of the saints around me glowed brilliantly in translucent light. The light that emanated from them was so pure that you could not help but be affected when near. Their sun-like appearance made it almost impossible to look directly at them. At the same time, it was hard not to be enthralled by the deep radiance.

Where some shone in unmasked light, many of the other saints glowed dimly as though something was shielding their light from shining. Curious to see what guarded the gleam from showing, I inched towards an older saint whose light seemed to be quenched.

I looked upon the veteran saint. The old man wore fatigue on his face. His body slouched as though he had fought too many battles in his lifetime. Over his chest he wore what looked like a hand-made vest. It was nothing special. It looked like it was made of worn-out leather that had been sown together and patched up time and time again. The word *Shame* was scratched right into the leather at the top of the vest. Following, was a long list of everything good and bad he had ever done since he was born.

I was about to begin talking to the old man when I felt a tap on my shoulder.

Turning around, I saw a familiar friend. "Journey?" I said surprised. "I thought I left you at the garden's entree."

Journey raised an eyebrow, "Ha! You think I would leave you alone in this place? Who knows what types of mischief you would get yourself into. Last time I let you do something by yourself, you put us behind schedule a year and three months. Whether you like it or not, I am coming with you."

I looked around and began to see how many people were actually wearing these different types of hand-made vests. There were multitudes of men, women and some children who were clothed in the ratted leather. All of which barely projected any light at all. Most who were dressed in these vests wore seriousness like a shield. Where if I were to be honest, their serious demeanor just made them look tired and joyless.

"Have you figured out what the leather vests are yet?" Journey tested.

I shook my head uncertainly.

Proceeding, Journey said, "The self-made vests are false breastplates of righteousness. Those who wear these plates have crafted them in their own strength and striving. They wear them believing that they will be received by God through their own works, instead of Christ's work. Little do they know, these vests actually veil their true splendor and potential from themselves and from others. These breastplates are the very thing which stops saints from shining in the same glorious image of God. The hope for this meeting is that those who are still striving for their own right standing with

God will lay down their own works to take on the true breastplates of righteousness."

He went on to say, "Many of the saints here are only visiting this garden for a time, where others will reside here for eternity in their hearts."

"Why would anyone want to leave this place?" I asked.

"Most leave because they do not think they are worthy to stay. Eventually they see that their works are useless and decide to leave. It is usually only those who encounter the Father and receive their name who learn to make the Garden of Intimacy their home. They learn to rest here because they understand that their value is not dependent on what they have done, but on who the Father says they are. Only those who learn to dwell in the Garden of Intimacy will wield the leaves that bring healing to the nations."

I could barely take in everything Journey was telling me. Everything here was a symbol for a deeper truth. Heaven was a feast for my understanding.

I wandered deeper into the sea of faces, noticing that the closer I got to the Tree of Life, the brighter the saints would shine. I could see in the distance that some of the saints were actually plucking leaves right from the Tree. One after another I would watch different shining saints boldly approaching the Tree. I watched a young boy who could not have been more than 11 years old walk up to the Tree of Life. He reached high and grabbed one of the golden leaves. Closing his eyes, he held the leaf to his chest as though it were precious and priceless to him. All of the glowing saints cheered and celebrated. Those who wore the fake breastplates of righteousness stood quietly for the most part. Those whose vests bore the word *Jealousy* scratched across the top looked angry. Those whose breastplates bore the word Flattery cheered along with those who shone; however, it seemed as though their heart posture was to draw attention to themselves instead of giving glory to God. All who wore the fake breastplates seemed to try and avoid the Tree at all costs. Most lingered at the back of the garden due to shame.

I suddenly saw someone cheering who struck a chord of familiarity in me. The woman's face had subtle similarities to a woman I had known years ago. She was a woman in her early fifties who attended a church that I once served. The woman was a new-born Christian and had a very infectious zeal for God and His kingdom. Only being one year old in the Lord, she passed away due to a sickness she had been battling for years. She now stood before me in her heavenly body, shining like a star. When I knew her on Earth she suffered from obesity, due to her sickness. In fact, I never knew her when she was well and healthy. Yet, here she gleamed radiantly. Just by looking at her I could tell that not a single speck of sickness or imbalance reigned in her being. She was whole. She was perfect.

Not looking the least bit surprised when she saw me, she greeted me with her famous sarcastic sense of humor, which apparently lived on with her into eternity. "Figured I would see you here sooner or later. Couldn't you have come to see me any faster?"

In the divine atmosphere around me, her casual talk seemed almost out of place. But then again, who ever said that Heaven was supposed to be overly serious? It was a place of life, celebration and joy after all. Needless to say, since I did not know how to respond I just laughed awkwardly. Behind me, I could hear Journey laughing under his breath as though he thought the scenario was amusing.

The woman's silky-white dress was ornamented in flawless pearls and diamonds. The glow on her face

The Great Summoning

contributed to her having the appearance of a bride prepared to meet her Bridegroom. "This is a wonderful place, isn't it?" she asked. "All of the splendor represented here is but a reflection of the Son of Man's glory."

As the woman spoke, I took notice of the fact that she cast no shadow. In fact, there were no shadows anywhere.

Before I could ask about this anomaly, my friend, obviously knowing what I was thinking began answering my question, "There are no shadows in Heaven. The Son of Man shines a light so bright that it has defeated even the subtleties of darkness. Have you noticed how it is forever morning here? There is no night. Though sorrow may last for the night, the joy comes in the morning. Night has been defeated and everlasting joy has taken its throne in our hearts. Tell me, have you met the Son of Man yet here in Heaven? You must meet Him. There is truly no one like Him. He is so exquisite a warrior that He fought Death itself in battle and won. He is such an insightful wise-man that He has uncovered secrets bound by mystery since before the foundations of the Earth were built. So great a King that He rules over every authority. One such as Him is born once throughout the entire course of history, you know. He is dangerous. Yet, He is the embodiment of everything that is good. There is hardly any point in you coming here if you do not encounter Love Himself."

"I want to encounter Him with everything in my being!" I blurted out.

A hearty laugh erupted from my friend. "And you soon will, I am sure."

I was fascinated by this woman's maturity. When I knew her on the Earth she was a new believer. In fact there were numerous times when I was the vessel God used to teach her fundamental truths of the cross. I had to ask her, "How is it that you have attained such revelation and maturity? I mean, I used to be one of your teachers, yet now your knowledge and understanding dwarfs mine."

Laughing again, she said, "With my heavenly body, my ability to understand is an ocean compared to the single drop of rain you, or any living person for that matter obtains."

As I tried to wrap my mind around her last statement, she switched topics. "Believe it or not, it is an honour to be talking to you right now. The Son of Man has commissioned me to intercede for you with Him until your time is done on Earth. It has been my utmost pleasure to do this. I can sense that you have recently been to the Mountain of Intercession. When you visited the onyx mountain, you got to experience your heart completely yoked to God's emotions for Heaven to invade Earth. In the same way, He has allowed my heart to be fully yoked to His desire for your life."

In that moment thankfulness struck me like a bolt of lightning. I felt so honoured to be covered in prayer to such a profound extent. I fell facedown to the ground and began worshipping the Lord. Everything in me worshipped Him. My friend who I conversed with also laid prostrate in worship to the one true God. I was consumed in the presence of God, lost in a timeless bliss of ecstasy.

I opened my eyes stirred by Journey's laugh. Looking up, I saw him talking to numerous different people; some who shone brightly, and others whose light was dimmed. Journey was such a social butterfly. I felt so honoured that someone so well-known and respected had befriended me. Journey's laugh was contagious to say the least. In fact I have never met someone who embodied joy so well. I was beginning to see that even if he had a serious task at hand, he seemed to be one who could always make it fun.

Getting up, I saw that my friend was gone. I felt disappointed that I had not gotten more time to converse with my old friend. I held in my heart everything she said, and knew that I would be forever moved by how honoured she was to continuously pray for me.

When Journey saw that I was up, he rushed over to me saying, "Nameless One! I want you to meet someone."

Journey wrapped a mighty wing around me and pulled me to come to one of the saints who he was having a conversation with. The man shone so brightly that I had to intentionally focus to distinguish facial features. However, when I did make out his countenance, I immediately knew who he was. The man did not look exactly the same as he did in the pictures I had seen of him in books. Just like Brother Lawrence and my friend who I had just met, he looked different because he was in his heavenly body instead of his earthly form. He was a saint who had already passed into eternity. I approached the man, not knowing that I was about to have a conversation that would change me forever. I reached out my hand, which was met by the hand of one of the greatest culture reformers ever known to man.

For the sake of confidentiality and honour I have decided to keep the man's name a secret. However, he was a Christian who undeniably brought forceful cultural change in the 1900's and was an activist for unity and for the restoration of human worth.

The man's face radiated joy. "It is an honour to meet you Nameless One!" He said with a laugh.

Are you kidding me? This spiritual giant knew who I was? I thought.

Laughing again he said, "You consider me a spiritual giant do you?"

"Why is it that everyone here can read thoughts except for me?" I asked.

"You also can, Nameless One, you just do not have the faith yet to do it. In Heaven there is no hiddenness of heart. Full transparency and trust has authority here, to the point where perfect unity between people exists."

I looked around to those who wore the false breastplates of righteousness. They seemed to only have surface level conversations and when they would fellowship, it was only with those who wore the same vests (other than those who were talking to Journey of course). Many however, just stood by themselves looking too afraid to talk to anyone at all. They seemed cut off from perfect unity, because who they truly were was buried underneath their works and striving. However, those who wore the true breastplates were a different story completely. These saints would at times actually walk right into one another, which made them look as though they became one person entirely. In Heaven you could actually step right into someone and understand them in full. Those who were clothed in light could experience the vast well of others throughout the army of saints.

The great activist continued, "Here we have a complete knowledge of one another. Nothing is hidden amongst family. We have full understanding concerning one another's past and present. Where we also know much about one another's future, only God has the complete picture and interpretation of what is to come. This is actually what my mandate was while I lived on the Earth. My heart was to bridge Heaven's perfect unity and acceptance to the world. Here no one is put down or placed on the outside, but each is fully received for who they were created to be. God's children are a diverse bunch, and every one of them was created to be loved and accepted."

As the great activist spoke, a single question engulfed my mind. "Tell me, if you had the chance to speak a message to those who are still living on the Earth, what would you tell them?"

The man answered as though he was prepared to give an answer to my question long before I even asked it. "Simple. I would tell them to accept everyone. There is a difference between accepting people versus accepting what they do. In order to revolutionize a culture you need to unflinchingly stand for what is morally right, bottom line. Do not shake from what the Spirit of God testifies is true, but love those who do. Give your life for them if it comes to it. This is what transforms culture, not pointing fingers. My life was threatened numerous times, and eventually was taken for the purpose of the unity of humankind."

"I would also tell this generation to lay down their lives for those who are overlooked, because in doing so they are sowing into greatness. One day the least likely will be some of your strongest leaders, since God always calls the foolish to shame the wise. If you overlook the prostitutes and the addicts, then you are overlooking some of your greatest upcoming leaders. Befriend the lowly and the friendless. Use your platform to raise up those who would have never had a chance to be seen or heard. Their voices are the ones which will bridge change and reformation to culture and society."

"Those of us who have already entered eternity know of every saint who walks the Earth. I knew of you long before Journey introduced you to me just now. You all have our full support, and you would be wise to heed the fact that even Paul the apostle rejoiced at the very thought of experiencing all that your generation of believers experiences now. It is an honour to live in the time period you live in."

I felt overwhelmed soaking in the wise words of the great revolutionist.

Right as I was about to ask another question, A booming voice interrupted my overwhelmed train of thought.

Even though I still was not even close to the front of the crowd that consisted of a multitude of people, I could clearly hear and see the one from whom the voice came. It was Gabriel. He was standing directly under the Tree of Life.

From Peasants To Royalty

Seeing Gabriel again struck a string of urgency in my spirit. I knew beyond any shadow of a doubt that something was about to happen that would change history forever.

Gabriel began, *"Saints of old and new. Angels of high ranks and low. I welcome you to the gathering that will mark history, and will forever be a sign in Heaven. You have all been called here that you might understand your importance in these last days. You have been called so that understanding concerning your identity may be broadened."*

To my right, the great revolutionist stood attentive, exuding nobility without even trying to. On my left stood Journey, who was becoming a beacon of familiarity to me. He was a solid pillar to my confidence, which continually reaffirmed to me that I belonged in this wonderful place.

Gabriel continued, *"There is one here whose testimony will bridge you into a greater revelation for your summoning."* Looking ahead, I saw Gabriel motioning for a young eight-year-old girl to come stand beside him beneath the golden Tree's mighty branches.

She stood in a simple green dress that was covered in flowers. The flowers looked as though they had been picked from the garden. On her head she wore a glimmering crown made from white gold. I could see the young girl's eyes widening as she saw the number of people she was about to speak to. The look on her face was not a look of fear; it was a look of wonder. She was taking in the moment, relishing in the privilege she had to share her story with such a group.

"He who has ears let him hear the word of the Lord," Gabriel proclaimed.

With a voice both sweet and soft, yet also bold, the girl began:

"I have a story. It is a story of suffering and sacrifice. But more than that it is a story of life and royalty."

Her voice was not as shaky as I assumed it would be. There was an undeniable confidence refined within her tone.

"Centuries ago my Papa and I were playing together in our home as Mama cooked supper. We lived in a small home. When we sat down to eat dinner we started to pray to Jesus, thanking Him for all that He has done for us. Thanking Him for His wonderful cross and for His glorious resurrection. Our prayers lingered longer than usual this night. Papa began to cry a bit as he talked to God. In a gentle voice he prayed, like God was his best friend. Suddenly we were interrupted when we heard men yelling from outside. My Papa gave my Mama a concerned look, then got up to see who was coming to our house. Our door all of a sudden burst open. The door hit my Papa, knocking him to the floor. I screamed so loud. My Mama rushed over to me and held me, crying. They began to hit my Papa and then my Mama and carried them out of our house. I was there all by

myself, when one of the bigger men came and grabbed me. I tried my hardest to get away but he was too strong."

"They threw us in a cage on wheels that had two other men in it. As they began driving us away from our home one of the men whispered to my Papa, 'They are taking us to the Colosseum; we do not have much time left.'"

"I knew what the Colosseum was. I overheard my Ma and Pa talking a few nights before about how men who did not know Jesus had been taking Christians to the Colosseum to kill them. At that thought I began to get dizzy and fell into my Papa's arms."

"I do not know how much time passed before I was awoken by a big bump in the road. Opening my eyes I saw a large building made of stone in the shape of a circle. I knew that this was where the men were bringing us. When we stopped, a man grabbed me and pulled me out of the cage with my family and the two men who were with us. They led us into the building and into a room with many other people. The room was dark and dirty. Everyone in the room looked very sickly and looked as though they had not eaten for a very long time. I could see people's bodily waste piled up in each corner."

"The room reeked."

"That night I laid on the cold, stone floor and cried silently. Mama always told me that God was with me; so I had to believe that He was. Even here, I knew He was. He was my best friend so I knew that He would never leave me. I closed my eyes and prayed that I would be strong for what was to come."

"Weeks passed. We only got a small portion of water each day and a piece of bread to share every two

or three days. I could tell that my Mama and Papa were getting skinnier. Once every week, five people were dragged out from the room. It was not even an hour after they were taken until we could hear crowds cheering followed by growls and screams."

"One morning, the men came into the room and made my Papa and Mama come with them. Mama cried real bad and I did too. As they left the room, a woman who had been there for only a few days held me tight.

"She whispered into my ear, 'be brave little one, be brave.'"

That day was the saddest day of my life. I did not know what was going to happen to my Mama and Papa, and part of me did not want to know."

"After that day, the woman who held me spent lots of time with me. She reminded me of my Mama. She would wipe my tears when I cried and would always tell me about how much Jesus loved me. She would tell me stories about what Heaven looked like and how I would meet Jesus in Heaven. I just needed to be brave."

"It was not too long before the men came to take me away. I was so weak at this point that I could not even fight to keep away from them. I could hear the woman who was my friend trying to help me, but she was not strong enough to keep the men away from me."

"They brought four others from the room with me and led each of us to smaller rooms by ourselves. In the room a man was sitting down at a single table. He motioned for me to sit down as well. The man had tears in his eyes and his voice was shaky when he spoke to me."

"He said to me, 'Child, we are going to give you an opportunity. If you deny Jesus then we will let you *live. However, if you fail to do this, then we will feed you to lions in front of a crowd of people. Your death will be their entertainment.'"*

"*Quietly the man began to speak to me, as though he was afraid of others hearing him. 'Please take the opportunity child... please.'*"

"*I felt so weak that I could hardly keep my eyes open. But I sat in silence thinking as hard as I could. I could never deny Jesus. He was everything to me. I had to be brave.*"

"*The man looked at me now with tears falling down his face. I knew that he wanted me to say it, but I could not. Two other men grabbed me by my wrists and began leading me out of the small room. They led me to a long hallway and commanded me to walk. Looking down the dusty hall was a giant wooden door that had light escaping through its cracks. That walk felt like the longest walk of my life. The farther I walked, the more people I could hear cheering and shouting. When the giant door finally opened, I saw the daylight for the first time in weeks. The crowds cheered even louder when they saw me. I could already see hundreds of people sitting in stands. When I heard the lions roaring, I screamed. I was so afraid! I was so afraid that I soiled myself. But I knew that I could do this. I knew that I could do this for Jesus because He was with me. I could be brave. I could be brave for Him.*"

"*I took a deep breath. Walked through the doors into the daylight and into eternity.*"

I looked over to Journey who looked as though he was reliving the story himself. The look upon his face was full of emotion. You could tell by his eyes that he was overwhelmingly proud of the young girl. He wore a simple, yet faint smile as if he were internally commending her for her bravery.

The girl continued speaking, *"I have told you before that my testimony is a story of suffering and sacrifice. But more than that it is a story of life and royalty. We need to understand that we are entering a new age of glory. We are crossing into a new season of identity. Jesus was not with me because I would give my life for Him. He was with me because He is my best friend. Many who follow Jesus live their lives as though they are peasants. They make decisions as though they are orphans. I could have denied my God, but I would have been rejecting my crown. I could have run away, but I would have been refusing my birthright."*

"You are all co-heirs to the throne of Heaven and Earth, yet you feel as though your royalty has been marred. I am here to tell you that it has not! Take off your peasant rags and be clothed with the robes that true kings and queens should wear! You are the kings and queens of creation! You are the sons and daughters of the living God! Take your thrones! Take up your scepters and crowns!"

The choir cheered and began to worship.

What a fascinating sight, I thought. *Men and women of God from all nations and all eras of history were assembled to sit under the counsel and testimony of an eight-year-old martyr. Even the hardest of hearts must have been shaken and moved by her passion.*

As the choir cheered and sang, Gabriel took his place underneath the Tree of Life once again. This time, standing behind him were five people, who I discerned were some of the pivotal living generals who would lead in the revival that was to take place. Three of the generals were women, and the remaining two were men. They were all adorned in splendorous battle gear and wore crowns of royalty on their heads. I could tell that sitting under the counsel of any of these five would be a priceless privilege.

"Sons and daughters of God," Gabriel began. *"Today will be a day of great freedom if you allow yourselves to submit to liberty. There are many Christians who have received Jesus as their Saviour, yet they have never truly met Him. You have the opportunity right now to lay down your false breast plates of righteousness to take up your full inheritance of rest and acceptance in Christ. Right now you are given the opportunity to encounter the Lord whenever you desire because your relationship with God will be built on the solid works of Jesus instead of your own. If you choose not to walk in freedom from dependence on your own works, this will not affect your salvation, for you have all professed the Lord as Saviour. However, your full potential and greatness will be veiled from you. For those of you who reject your freedom there will be a time, perhaps after your ascension, when you realize that your own stubbornness and pride was the very thing that prevented you from making your most profound mark for the Kingdom of Heaven. Yet, for those of you who take this opportunity, you will begin a journey of experiencing the never-ending benefits of your birthright. Neither shame nor pride will hold power over you, forcing you into patterns of lack nor complacency. You will instead sail upon the golden wings of the Lord, adventuring into the boundless blessings of God. Understand that lives throughout the nations literally hang on the balance of your present decision."*

Silence reigned throughout Heaven for a moment. But how long the moment actually lasted, I could not tell you. It was timeless. Delicate. It could have lasted three seconds or hundreds of years for all I know.

Eventually shining hands from throughout the crowd began rising into the air in worship. I watched as different saints who wore the false breastplates lifted their hands as well. As they did, bright lightning bolts shot from the Tree of Life and shattered the leather vests off of their chests. I could hear the sound of the false breastplates of righteousness breaking from every direction of the garden. Right as the old breastplates were broken, new breastplates of gold were revealed on each person. Set in the plates were innumerable flawless gem stones. The light that shone from the freed saints was breathtaking. Some who received their freedom immediately went up to pluck leaves from the Tree of Life, which were for bringing healing to the nations.

Even though many experienced this liberty, I could see others who sadly still wore their manmade vests. As the shining ones cheered in celebration, the leather-bound vest bearers stood quietly, worshipping their own works with their silence.

Even though my heart was utterly broken for the false breastplate bearers, it was impossible for me not to worship the living God. Even amidst the great compassion I had for these people, joy reigned. Joy was the dominant force and it was impossible to quench. The army of the Lord began to dance in celebration. Several men and women danced a dance of their cultures. Different tongues of men and angels praised and laughed undignified.

A song of praise resounded from the army in unison. I sang along with them:

"The Son of Man now shines His light,
revealing long forgotten names.
The orphan children now in white,
presented forth in royal fame."

"The solid Rock has stolen shame,

refining confidence to stone.
The Tree of Life will shake its mane,
to blanket Earth with leaves of gold."

As we all worshipped, I began to see an angel in the distance who looked like a small child pushing through the crowd in my direction. The angel held my attention; however, after watching it for a time, I closed my eyes and continued worshipping.

When I opened my eyes again, the angel was standing directly in front of me. The angel looked like a messenger from the 1700's. His cherub face resembled that of a six-year-old boy. This angel was so boy-like that if I had not discerned that this was an angel, I would have easily mistaken him for a small child.

"Are you Nameless One?" The angel asked.

I nodded my head to say 'yes'.

The angel then continued, "I have been looking for you everywhere. The High-General of all of Heaven's army has asked to see you in His private tent."

I looked around and spotted Journey watching the angel and I converse. By the knowing smirk on his face, I knew exactly who the High-General was.

I was going to see the Son of Man.

Secrets Unfold

By the small angel's leading, I found the General's tent. It was not an enormous tent by any means. It was a moderate size, even somewhat small, made from beige and light brown fabrics. The tent was not all that spectacular and seemed to be crafted purposefully normal. It was set up east from the Tree of Life, stationed in front of a hill that led to the many other places in the Garden of Intimacy. Saints from the army passed by the seemingly insignificant meeting place, oblivious to the fact that the most important person who had ever walked the Earth dwelled in that very tent.

"Some people live their lives dreaming of visiting this tent, Nameless One. However it can only be found by those who are invited. It is a great honour to be here," Journey explained to me.

The angel stood by the tent's doorway, holding the flap open for me to enter. Journey and I ducked in. The layout of the inside of the tent looked just as unimpressive as the outside. There were old scrolls piled up all over the tent and in the very middle of the meeting place was a wooden desk with two wooden chairs. However, behind the desk stood One who was by no means ordinary. Standing before me was the High-General of all Heaven's army. The Son of Man. Jesus.

A Timeless Journey

I had contemplated many times before how I would react when I met Jesus face to face. Would I dance? Sing? Weep? Instead, I stood wide-eyed and unmoving, not knowing how to respond. My eyes welled with tears as I looked upon the most beautiful man I had ever seen. It was not necessarily His appearance that made Him beautiful, because other than being clad in the attire of a General, He looked quite normal. It was His heart that moved me so. This was the Man who made life worth living.

I felt peace, joy, love, compassion, awe, inspiration and admiration all at the same time. How could I pick a single way to react when I was experiencing every positive emotion that existed? I just stood at the entrance looking at Him with my hands behind my back, trying my best to be perfectly postured. He was a General after all. I waited for His instruction.

Jesus met my gaze with a serious look and stared into me. Panic hit me immediately. The King of kings was looking directly at me. He let a very uncomfortable silence linger. My mind raced. Why wasn't He saying anything? Does He want me to say something? Does He want me to do something? He must know that I feel uncomfortable.

As Jesus continued staring, His bottom lip began to quiver. Not being able to hold it in any longer, He burst out laughing. Journey laughed as well. I was starting to find it interesting how Journey seemed to make me the centre of His amusement. I laughed along awkwardly, still unsure of what was going on.

Jesus walked around the table still laughing. He gave me a big hug and kissed me right on the cheek. Finally feeling at ease, I let the tension in me drop.

Jesus spoke, "Sorry, but I couldn't resist. The look on your face was hilarious. I am glad to see that you have responded to my call. Do you have any idea why I have invited you here?"

"I honestly have no clue," I responded.

"I have brought you here because I want to share with you my strategy for revival in the nations for this age."

I gulped. "Why did you choose me? I mean... I don't even know who I am. I don't even know my own name. Aren't there others who would be better qualified? You know, people who are better equipped?"

"Of course there are," Jesus said bluntly. "However, that is why I have chosen you. Look around at all of the scrolls that surround us. These are the strategies I have shared with my prophets ever since the foundations of the Earth were built. Countless men and women of God have met in this very tent, many whose names you yourself would know. Many whose lives you have studied. Many of those men and women of God began as the vilest of sinners. Some were murderers. Others were adulterers. But, they were all men and women after my own heart. They were men and women who honoured the secret place with me above all things. This is how I choose who should be entrusted with important strategy and revelation. I choose the foolish to shame the wise. I have a reputation of calling those who feel like nothing, and turning them into someone important. I am the author of hope and destiny. I am the restorer of purpose and life."

A feeling of both importance and humility washed over me. Words that Brother Lawrence shared with me on the Mountain of Intercession ran through my head, *"What you just experienced when you drank water from the River of Revelation is what every ministry, or life for that matter, should be built upon. It should be built upon a non-stop intimate encounter with the heart of*

God. Many build their lives upon a philosophy, doctrine or principal. Yet, wisdom beckons us to build life upon a person, the Son of Man."

Overwhelmed, I was just barely able to push words past the lump in my throat. "What is Your strategy Lord? Can I see the scroll for this age?"

Jesus laughed, "I love your boldness. However, I am not going to tell you just yet. You are acting far too militant for my liking."

Jesus pulled out a wooden chair for me. "Come sit down at my desk with me."

When I sat, Jesus walked around to the other side and took a seat as well. He then opened a drawer from His desk and pulled out two things. First, He pulled out a scroll and unrolled it on the desk. The scroll was a map of the world. Golden letters were written over each nation, city, town, island and village. Secondly, Jesus pulled out a deck of cards. He began dealing.

"I will instead tell you like this," Jesus said as He tossed cards onto the rolled out scroll. "Just because I am a General, does not mean I need to be militant in every way. Understand this, I tell my secrets only to my friends. I would not be able to trust a simple warrior with my deepest and most important secrets, even though the title of a warrior is a noble title indeed. I share my secrets with those who have waited on me and have taken time to learn my personality, character and heart. Those are the ones who truly understand my friendship."

As we played cards, Jesus shared with me His heart and strategy for the nations. He read much of the golden script that was full of declarations over different nations, cities, towns, islands and villages. However, He did not read the entire golden script to me, explaining that He would share the rest with others since all are to know and prophesy only in part. As He meticulously unfolded a strategy of revival, we laughed and bonded together. Jesus then told me that I would share this strategy with those He selects throughout the entire course of my life, but not to share it with a single person until He Himself tells me to do so.

When Jesus rolled up the scroll, the same small angel who had led me to the tent walked into the entry way. Following him were five saints. I immediately recognized them as the five generals who stood with Gabriel under the Tree of Life. The five projected undeniable confidence in their royal identity. They were kings and queens of Heaven and Earth, and they knew it. One of the women stepped forward: "You have summoned us Lord?"

"Yes, I have my dear friends. I wanted to introduce you to another friend of mine here." Jesus motioned to me. "I have given him pivotal revelation concerning the upcoming revival that will sweep throughout the nations. I wanted to introduce you to him now in Heaven, because you will all eventually meet him on Earth."

Each general looked pleased, yet at the same time there was a look on a few of their faces that gave the impression that they all held an unspoken question concerning what Jesus had just told them.

Jesus, discerning their thoughts, responded before they could even ask, "Yes, I know. He is quite young, isn't he?" Jesus quipped playfully. "Before you mention his youthfulness, you should know that I have chosen a youth on purpose. This generation of youth will show vast depths in wisdom and insight. In fact, you will soon be seeing young apostles and prophets stepping into governance roles over entire churches at very young ages. Even in their 20's they will wield wisdom greater than those in their 60's. This will come to pass because we are in accelerated times, and although it seems foolish in the world's sight for youth to be entrusted with much, it is logical in mine."

Jesus looked at me affectionately, "I love you, my friend. The five generals and I have great deeds to take care of here and the Spirit of Revelation is beckoning for you to grow deeper into understanding. Your time in this meeting place is done for now. I will call you here again when the time is right. You will see me again shortly in the Hall of Mantles."

I stepped towards Jesus, gave Him a hug and let Him kiss me on the cheek again. Turning around towards the tent's exit, Journey placed a wing on my back and walked out with me to step onto the Garden's perfect grass once again.

I watched men and women walking past the normalized tent, completely oblivious to its hidden greatness. "I have never experienced intimacy like that before, Journey. I don't think there is anything that could top what I just experienced in that tent."

Questioning me, Journey responded, "Oh no? What if I told you that I am going to take you to see the Father next?"

My heart stopped. I was finally going to know my name.

A Love That Is Wild

"How far of an expedition is it to the Father?" I asked Journey.

"Closer than you would think." With one of his wings, Journey pointed, "You see that hill behind the tent where Jesus and the five generals are meeting? The Father is right over that hill. He is there regularly. It is one of His favourite places."

"Why is it one of His favourite places?"

Journey looked at me, "You know, your ability to ask questions is one of your best qualities, Nameless One. However, you will see for yourself soon enough."

"Fair enough," I said laughing lightly. "I am really looking forward to when you stop calling me Nameless One, by the way."

Journey just smiled.

We began walking up the hill together. As I climbed, butterflies were making my stomach turn. Why am I nervous? I thought. Am I afraid that I will be rejected? What if the Father does not receive me for who

I am? What if He does not even like me as a person? Even though my mind was trying to convince me to turn right back around and go back down the hill, my legs kept moving. It felt like eternity getting to the top of that hill, and when I finally did, I saw something that I did not expect.

Journey and I sat on the top of the hill together, watching the marvelous scene unfolding before us. In the middle of a grand field was the Father dancing hand in hand with a little girl who could not have been more than four years old.

The Father had a look of deep affection on His face as He danced with her. At times He would pick the girl right up off of the ground, embrace her in a deep hug and then spin her in a circle. The Father looked exactly as I assumed He would. He was the most unthreatening person I have ever seen. He wore what looked like white linen and His long hair and beard were as white as snow. Even though He had a head full of white hair there was a youthfulness about Him. Someone who is eternal seems more young than old.

As the little girl danced with the Father, there was an unforgettable look in her young eyes. It was a look someone possessed only when they understood that they truly belonged. With each step, with every twirl and spin, you could see that an understanding was forming within her. It was an understanding that she was fully accepted as a daughter. You could tell that the question of whether or not He loved her did not even exist to her.

Journey then spoke, "You know, when you know the Father, even though your body gets older, your spirit gets younger. It gets younger because you get to become like a child, forever growing into the revelation that you are truly loved, received and celebrated, just as you are."

A Love That Is Wild

Around the Father and the four year old girl, were millions of other children waiting for their turn to dance with Him. They all stood with smiles on their youthful faces, gazing upon the endearing sight. The love that the Father had towards each of these children was so mighty that not one single child felt restless or jealous waiting for their turn. Not one felt left out or overlooked by Him. Being around the Father, each knew that they were loved and received by Him completely. They all waited patiently for their turn, excited for each child that He danced with.

"Have you figured out who all these children are?" Journey asked me.

"I haven't the slightest clue," I responded quietly, too moved to speak any louder.

Journey shared, "These are all of the children who have ever been aborted throughout the entire course of history. The world said that they did not even exist, yet the Father spends much of His time here showing these children that they have a parent who loves them. They have a Father who loves them."

This was too much for me to take in. I sat, moved in a way that I had never thought possible. The children's eyes glimmered, full of life. They were truly happy. They truly felt as though they belonged. I watched as the Father lavished His love upon each child. Watched as He made each one understand that they were the centre of His world. Not only did the children seem moved by this experience, but the Father Himself seemed just as moved, if not more so. These children were everything to Him. They were His joy. His love was so great towards them that every time a child would smile at Him, or even look at Him, you could tangibly feel His heart leap in excitement. Love such as this was nearly unfathomable to me. It was both precious and priceless.

As I became lost in the moment, Journey talked on, "The Father told me Himself that there would one day be mass funerals for all of the children who were murdered through abortion. Entire nations will come to their senses and repent for the terrible wrong that has been done. These will be glorious days and a wonderful victory. This will begin a movement where human life will be valued on a much greater scale."

I felt as though I was frozen still in one place. Part of me felt like crying because of the sheer beauty of the Father's love towards these children. Another part of me wanted to begin interceding then and there for the end of abortion. The death of dehumanization, what a wonderful thought. Instead of doing either, I just watched the Father lavishing His love upon each child.

Only a brief amount of time passed before Journey began prodding me. "So, are you going to go and meet Him?"

"What?" I asked, pretending to sound surprised by Journey's question. Really, I had already been contemplating it before he asked. Everything in me wanted to meet the Father. Yet I knew in my heart that I would not be able to bring myself to approach Him. Everything in me wanted to be with Him. To dance with Him as these children did. To be held in a deep hug by Him. To belong. But there was a part of me that feared He would reject me. Part of me preferred not to know who I was instead of risking disappointment or hurt.

"Another time, Journey. I just don't feel ready."

A few seconds passed when I realized that I heard no reply.

"Journey?"

A Love That Is Wild

I looked over in his direction and saw that he was gone. "Journey?!"

What an odd occurrence. Ever since I met Journey, he had refused to leave my side. Getting up off the ground, I looked around. He was nowhere to be seen. I needed to find him. Grief filled me, knowing that I would have to leave this wonderful sight to find the missing bird. Looking at the Father one last time, I sighed.

Knowing that this was not the last time I would see Him, I turned around and started my descent down the hill to find my old friend, Journey.

Falling Into Understanding

While descending down the hill, I could hear numerous voices speaking authoritatively all at once. I could see the five generals giving orders to the saints from underneath the Tree of Life. These were the five generals who I met in the tent of meeting.

Many of the saints were assembled into different groups. A variety of angels were grouped with the saints, listening intently. It seemed as though even they followed instruction from the five. Every once and a while, one of the five would give specific instructions to the different angels. Those angels who received the commands would fly right out of Heaven to different cities and nations in the Earth.

"Journey?!" I yelled. I wandered along the outskirts of the garden aimlessly, looking for the missing eagle. Even though I could not see Journey, I still felt his lingering presence.

As I searched, I could overhear different saints throughout the army muttering about the Hall of Mantles. The Hall of Mantles was the very place where Jesus told me that I would go to meet with Him again.

A Timeless Journey

While trying to imagine what the Hall might look like, my attention was grabbed by a particular youth, who was walking from group to group very stealthily, carrying a notepad. Although I wanted to find Journey, there was something in me that knew that I needed to talk to this youth. Weaving throughout the army of saints yet again, I made my way to the young boy.

When I finally reached the boy, I could tell that my presence immediately caught his eye. The boy confidently reached out his hand to shake mine. Even though this boy seemed to have the appearance of a 12 year old, he was clothed as a king. Both his crown and robe were subtle, yet they held tremendous weight and authority. He had a scepter strapped onto his back, easy to access if need be, and a golden leaf from the Tree of Life pinned onto his royal vest. Being around the boy, I could feel a profound integrity radiating from him that exceeded my own. I reached out my own hand to meet his, which was both small and delicate.

"Who are you?" I asked.

The boy gave me a mild smirk. "I am one of the upcoming apostolic leaders in the nations," he responded. "I must say that I am very impressed that you allowed me to be highlighted to you. Most overlook what I carry because of my age."

I took the subtle compliment. "Why is it that you are running from group to group?" I asked.

"I am observing what the five general are saying and doing with each group of saints. I am trying my best to learn through observation so that I may walk in a greater maturity when I step into my ordained apostolic office. The different groups are different churches, ministries and those who are called to specific movements in different regions. The five have been going from group to group, bringing church government into alignment. Would you like to come with me?"

I knew that there was something I needed to receive from this young warrior of God. I could feel a weighty teaching beginning to unfold.

"I would love to!" I said with zealous excitement.

The youthful leader led me to a group that had no more than 50 people. At the group's front, there was a man and woman who each held a shepherding rod. They were obviously the leaders of this ensemble of saints. As I observed the other groups from a distance, it seemed to be very common to have leaders such as them. The troupe had a variety of different people. However, most just wore simple peasant clothes. There was one man who had a sheath strapped to his waist that held a sword that looked as though it had not been drawn for years. About half of the group seemed overweight, where the other half seemed to suffer from malnutrition. You could see an obvious gauntness in their faces.

The young boy spoke, "I have seen this before. Not every time, but often this can happen when a church has a pastoral covering instead of an apostolic covering."

Right then, one of the males of the five generals came to the group. As soon as he came, you could instantly feel a new sense of stability amongst the saints. It was a stability that, instead of fearing healthy change, invited it.

I looked around, trying to spot Journey, yet he still seemed to be missing. Even though I could not see or hear him, I allowed myself to be stilled in his presence that was still evident.

A Timeless Journey

The first thing the general-apostle did was honour the two pastors for tending the group so well. He embraced them both in a hug and had the group applaud the man and woman for serving so diligently. The general began a short-winded speech. "Brothers and sisters, I am honored to be with you today. For a very long time, your pastors have served this church diligently as shepherds and have done an excellent job in doing so. However, the bulk of the ministerial burden has fallen on their shoulders and now they suffer from burnout. Your pastors have called me to bring order and proper government to this church."

Saints began looking at one another in bewilderment by the notion of such a sudden shift. The general continued, "My heart is to train you all to be open gates for Heaven to be manifested through. As an apostle, I will do things that will cause you to rejoice, but I will also do things that you will not understand at first. In these times I encourage you to trust me as your leader instead of allowing offense to swell towards me."

The group then began to clap and shout in agreement. I was relieved to see the saints so willing to submit to their new leadership. The young boy and I watched as the refined apostle then began going from saint to saint, placing a crown on the head of each. Every crown looked different, crafted personally for each saint. As he placed a crown upon each head, peace and joy intoxicated every person. Sobriety of identity brought clarity to each. I knew right away in my spirit that these were no ordinary crowns. I was actually beginning to see Ephesians 6 unfolding right before my eyes. These crowns were actually helmets of salvation. This apostle was granting them security in what Jesus did on the cross.

The apostle then went around to every saint, placing a breastplate of righteousness on those who did not yet wear one. To those who already wore a true breastplate, he made sure that every single one was properly secured and fastened. The saints who formerly looked like peasants were beginning to reflect their true identities. An authentic trust was beginning to take shape towards their leader.

I looked over at the young boy, seeing that he was furiously taking notes.

Then the apostle did something that no one expected. He called forth a man from the congregation who wore a blue cloak and had the sheathed sword hanging at his side. You could feel the weight of importance when he was called up. Those in the group watched the cloaked man both curiously and cautiously. The apostle then spoke authoritatively, "This man has been called as a gift to your church, yet you have rejected him because of your fear of the unknown. He has been hidden in your congregation, waiting for your hearts to be ripened to receive his words. This man will walk alongside of me as I establish a firm foundation amongst you. He will also take part in training and equipping you. I introduce to you, the lead prophet of this house."

When the apostle introduced the prophet, tension built up quickly between the group and the apostle. Many began to scoff and complain. At the mention of a prophet, a look of sheer terror came upon the two pastor's faces.

"I told you that you must trust me as a leader, even when you do not understand," the apostle said. *"In order for this house to reach maturity, you need the prophetic ministry active amongst you."*

When the apostle engaged in healthy confrontation with the group, I was impressed to see the two pastors intentionally shake terror and offense from their faces. However, some from the group did not have such an immediate change of heart. Many began walking away and going to other groups. The loss of people did not seem to sway the apostle in the slightest. In fact, it looked as though he expected as much. The apostle then turned the platform to the prophet to speak. Before the prophet spoke, he pulled his sword out of his sheath and then lifted it into the air. Many gasped in wonder. As the prophet shared God's heart for the church his words were vibrant. The atmosphere became pregnant with vision.

Even though the Spirit of God was clearly moving, even more people left the group. In total only 23 remained. But, those who remained had a much greater passion and solidity to them. Once the people were refreshed by new vision and guidance, they were confident in their leadership once again.

The cloaked prophet then went out to the remaining 23, handing out similar swords to what he himself carried. These swords were the swords that are written about in Ephesians 6. These swords were the word of God, which every saint now carried instead of only the prophet.

As the prophet was going around teaching people to wield their new swords, the apostle brought in a new member to the leadership team. This person was not one of the five generals, but was a short man who carried a scroll under his arm. When the apostle introduced him as the church's teacher, looks of delight swept across each saint's face. The apostle clarified, *"The teacher will bring a proper balance to the prophet's ministry in our church, just as the prophet will bring proper balance to the teacher's ministry. Receive him well. The teacher's ministry binds the whole armor of God together in such a way that it can be worn with integrity and excellence."*

Falling Into Understanding

The teacher then began to speak, showing how everything that the apostle and prophet did amongst them was entirely scriptural. As he taught, any remaining tension towards leadership ceased to exist. He then went around placing the belt of truth around each saint's waist. As he did, those who suffered from malnutrition began bulking up. The gauntness in their faces filled in. Numbers again began to increase to about 70 people as the teacher began walking in his role.

As the prophet and teacher went around imparting and training, the two pastors went around processing with each person concerning everything that was taking place. After they did this for a time, the apostle called the two over to him. The young boy and I crept up to the three to hear what they were talking about.

The apostle said to them, *"You two have done an excellent job in shepherding the sheep; however, I have a greater tool that will help you to pastor on a greater scale."* The apostle then pulled a shield out from behind his back. *"This is the shield of faith with which you will be able to quench all the fiery darts of the wicked one. Go amongst the saints teaching them about their sonship and daughtership. Teach them how to receive healing in their souls, so that not a single lie or dart can penetrate the shields of faith they receive from your ministry."* The pastors then went out handing out shields of faith to each saint.

Lastly the apostle brought in a woman who carried a great ram's horn. This woman had an intense passion about her and a violent love for people. *"This woman will be the evangelist of this house,"* The apostle proclaimed. *"Without her ministry in the church, you will never fulfill your mandate."*

The evangelist then went about placing on each saint's feet shoes that were the preparation of the gospel of peace. As the evangelist did this, those who were overweight in the group began to decrease in size because the word of God in them became active. The group then began to grow drastically to about 500 people. The majority of new people did not come from other groups. Instead, they began materializing into Heaven out of nothing as though they were being birthed as new creations right into Heaven.

Each saint was now adorned for the battle of the Lord. Each was equipped to release and wield the Kingdom of Heaven. After stationing numerous leaders throughout the group to steward the move of God that was taking place, the apostle gave his word that he would be back to impart, and would always play a role of governance in the church. The apostle then went to another group to bring proper order such as he did with this one.

"I have never seen a church brought into such order so quickly!" I said to the young boy.

"That is how an apostle's gift often works," the young boy said. "However, it took much longer than you thought. That may have only felt a few hours of change here in Heaven, but what you just saw will take 34 years to unfold on Earth. Reformation can take time, yet it is well worth it. A Sarah anointing is about to rest on the church. God is going to be training churches who are even 90 years of age to give birth to revival. In order for this to happen, reformation must take place. These churches will carry the wisdom of the aged to steward these moves of God, yet will walk in a youthful zeal to keep it fresh and present."

The 12 year old boy's eyes darted to where the general-apostle was now ministering. "I must be going now, Nameless One, before I miss what the apostle does with the next group. Will you be coming with me?"

Falling Into Understanding

    I wanted to go with him to expand my knowledge of church reformation, but my longing beckoned me to find Journey. "I'm sorry, but I have to find a friend of mine," I said.

    "Very well then, farewell!" the young-upcoming leader said as he chased after the seasoned apostle.

    I began walking away from the different groups of saints, now wandering along the outskirts of the Garden. Behind me, the generals, saints and angels went about their tasks meticulously. As thankful as I was to learn what I had in the Garden's main court, I felt relieved to be out of its hectic environment for the time being.

    Faintly looking around, my eyes spotted a place in the garden that I had not yet seen before. Behind a division of trees was a section that branched off from the Garden's main court. Leading into what looked like a secret room was a subtle cobblestone path. Much like the tent where Jesus and the five met, people seemed to just walk past not giving it any attention at all. Without hesitation I followed the trail and slipped into the Garden's hidden room that was walled by trees.

    The section was just as immaculate as the grand court, if not more so, but was much smaller and completely private. The small inner court was dressed in flowers. Every species of flower I had ever seen on Earth was represented here, and many others that were entirely new to me. The fragrance was intoxicating. Even though Heaven's army was only a few hundred feet away, stillness had authority in this place. There was not a whisper of sound in the inner court. I sat in this personalized-miniature garden and began to soak in the glorious presence of God that enshrouded it.

With my back turned from the entrance, I heard graceful footsteps come in from behind me. Before I could turn, I heard a reassuring voice. "Nameless One…"

Turning around, I blurted out, "Journey! Where have you…" At the sight of him I stopped.

It was Journey's voice, yet his appearance had changed. Instead of a great eagle, a majestic stallion was standing before me. The mighty horse was whiter than the whitest of snow. I looked into the stallion's eyes to meet the endearing green and orange colours that pierced my soul the first time I met Journey.

"Journey, what happened to your appearance?"

"I can take whatever appearance I need to, Nameless One. In fact, I will take whatever role in your life that you need me to, depending on your season. Where your last season was a time of journeying into understanding, I led you as a journeyman. This next season in your life is a season of freedom; therefore, I will lead you into freedom and restoration. This way in due time you will have the confidence to approach the Father. As your mentor, I will lead you in all ways."

Perplexed I said, "Should I begin calling you Freedom instead of Journey now?"

The stallion smiled. "You still do not know who I am, do you? Journey and Freedom are not names, they are only titles you have known me by. This is not even my true form. I have simply taken these forms so that you would have a grid to relate to me. I am a person."

As he said this, he began taking on a new form once again. Every part of Him changed except for His loving eyes. However, the appearance He took, I could not describe with earthly words even if I wrote thousands of pages in an attempt to illustrate Him. He was indeed a person. Standing on the secret place's perfect grass, He was dressed in humility, yet the atmosphere around Him was so intense that it was undeniable that He was the possessor of the very power that created the Heavens and Earth.

Speaking again, He said, "This is my true form, and this is how you will know me from this point on. I am the person who Jesus promised would come to co-labour with humankind on the Earth after He ascended. I am all things to you. I am your Teacher, your Comforter and closest friend; you just didn't know it."

"I am Holy Spirit."

From Deep To Deep

All this time, without me even knowing it, the personality of the Godhead was walking side by side with me throughout this entire adventure. Now I knew why His eyes burned into me like fire. I understood why He felt like more than a friend to me. He conversed so well with everyone throughout the army of saints because He was their Teacher and Counsellor as well. Revelation rested upon me as I finally grasped why Jesus said that it would be better for Him to leave, so that Holy Spirit could come. Holy Spirit was part of me. He was my best of friends. His name was not *Journey*, or *Freedom*. His name was Holy Spirit.

Something within me began stirring wildly. An overwhelming love toward Holy Spirit took me. I ran up to Him and hugged Him with all my might. Holy Spirit began to laugh. As He held me, I could feel His power enshrouding me. Holy Spirit was wordless as He held me. However, through His gentle touch, His love for me was communicated flawlessly.

What a wonderful place to be, I thought.

A Timeless Journey

As Holy Spirit held me in an embrace, a question began to flood my mind. I had to ask Him, "Holy Spirit, why is it that you left me when we were watching the Father together?"

Even though I could not see Holy Spirit's face, I could feel Him smiling. "Come and take a seat with me, Nameless One."

Holy Spirit laid upon the secret garden's grass with His hands folded behind His head. I did the same. As I looked up to the sky, even though I was gazing upon morning skies, the stars shone in plain sight before me, sparkling like distant torches. Never had I believed that I could see so many stars in broad daylight.

As soundless minutes lingered I had the opportunity to take in the intimacy of the moment. With a tone that was filled with affection toward me, Holy Spirit broke the silence. "I have never left you, friend. I will never leave you nor forsake you. Even though you could not see or hear me for a time, could you not feel my presence?"

"Of course I did. It felt as though You were right by my side," I remarked.

"There will be times when my voice seems loud and times when I seem more silent, yet I am always with you. This shift takes place because there are seasons of mandate as well as seasons of invitation. There are times when I will tell you exactly what to do and how to do it. There will be other times when I will give you invitation to do something how you choose. This is all part of walking in friendship with me. My job is not to just tell you what to do. My role in your life is far greater than that. I am your Teacher. My job is to teach you how to walk in the mind of Christ. If I made every decision for you then you would never know how to lead and reign with confidence."

"When you could not see or hear me, I was testing you to see what decision you would make when you felt prompted to talk to the young, apostolic child. You made an excellent choice in following him. You were following my leading without even knowing it. My heart is to equip you to think the way that a son would think. I desire to train you to make the same decisions that Jesus Himself would make. A father will hold his son's hand when he is young. This is because children cannot yet make wise decisions on their own. They need to be taught what is right from wrong. They need to be taught what is wise and what is foolish. The father's job is to train his child how to make the right decisions so that the child's ignorance does not echo into adulthood. As the boy becomes a man, he should not have to be walked by the hand throughout every situation, because through proper parenting his mind is reformed to think the way his father thinks. However, even in the responsibility of adulthood a son would be wise to heed his father's voice. This is an important key concerning how to be yoked with me. This is a revelation that will empower you in how to reign with Christ in maturity."

"You are to be trained by me to the extent that you can be trusted to do the work of the Kingdom with great influence. Understand that I am your Helper, not your doer. Always remember, you must walk through the Garden of Intimacy to get to the Tree of Life. Once you get to the Tree, then you can receive the leaves that bring healing to the nations. You will never get to the Tree to fetch the leaves unless you understand intimacy with me and the importance of my presence. That being said, there are many who know how to walk through the Garden of Intimacy with me, yet do not know how to wield the leaves to bring healing to the nations once they get to the Tree. In order to see mass Kingdom invasion on the Earth, you must understand both intimacy and how to reign. You must understand that you are both a priest and monarch in order to make royal decisions."

As Holy Spirit spoke I could feel something solidifying within me. His words felt like seeds being planted directly into my heart. These were seeds that would never die or drown even if they were confronted by a thousand storms.

"Can I tell you something Holy Spirit?" I asked.

"Of course. What is on your mind?"

"Well... I feel regret since I did not have the confidence to go and meet the Father. I mean, He was right there. There could not have been a better opportunity. How am I supposed to fully understand who I was created to be if I fear the only person who can tell me who I am?"

As I was sharing my heart, Holy Spirit was fully attentive, weighing each word I spoke. He was indeed the great Counselor. "There is no need to feel regret, Nameless One. Many believers go their entire lives without meeting the Father. It is quite unfortunate, because they are missing out on love in its purest form. But this is why I am walking with you. I am going to lead you into freedom, so that you may not only meet Him, but also know Him as you know the Son of Man and me. The Father is in everything good that you see, Nameless One. He is not far, but at hand."

"Why is it that people fear approaching Him? He seemed so non-threatening and meek. What do I need to do to have the confidence?"

"The answer to your question is incredibly simple, friend. You need to learn to trust. You need to learn how to take the Father's word for who He says He is. You need to trust who the Son of Man and I say He is. We are One with Him you know. Why do people fear approaching the Father, you ask? Take yourself for instance: You feared approaching Him because you feared He would turn you away. You feared that He would reject you because you assumed that you would not be good enough to receive His love. You need to stop trusting your assumptions of Him based off of your own past hurtful experiences in relationships. Trust Him for who He is. Once you can trust Him with your whole heart, then you will be ready to truly know Him."

Holy Spirit's answer was direct, but not even remotely harsh. Each word He spoke was coated in love and gentleness. I sat up slowly, and looked over to Him. "Holy Spirit, you said that you and the Father are One. Who is it that you say He is?"

A smile came upon Holy Spirit's face as glorious as the sun's rise, and He said, "The Father is love. He is acceptance and refuge. He is power and gentleness. I tell you the truth, Nameless One, never in all of eternity has the Father turned away a single child when they have come to Him. And He never will. That is who He is. When you can learn to believe Me, you will be ready to meet Him."

I laid my head down on the perfect grass again, pondering Holy Spirit's words.

"Your time to meet Him will come before you know it," Holy Spirit said. "Before then, there are great truths' that you must comprehend. There are extraordinary sights that your eyes need to behold."

Holy Spirit then invited intimately, "Close your eyes, Nameless One, I want to show you something."

Knowing that Holy Spirit had proven Himself to be trusted time and time again, I shut my eyes without even thinking about it. For the first few seconds, absolute stillness filled my ears. I was consumed by it.

I then started to hear wind subtly begin to howl, which seemed out of character for the small garden. The wind grew louder and louder. With my eyes still shut, I was discerning that my surroundings were beginning to shift and change. The ground beneath me even took on a different feel. It no longer felt soft and cozy, but instead was as hard as stone.

Before I could ask Holy Spirit what was going on, He told me to open my eyes. As I opened them, I saw that the Secret Place had completely disappeared. Not a single blade of grass, flower or tree was in sight. The still quiet of the garden was now replaced by a howling wind. In the sky were still millions of stars. However the stars looked as though they were ordered differently, confirming that I was in a new place entirely.

Looking over to Holy Spirit, He held a casual look upon His face. Instead of resting in the perfect inner court, I now laid suspended thousands of feet in the air upon a mountain that was made entirely of diamond.

The Creator's Heart

I watched the diamond shimmer under the sun's radiance. If I looked at parts of the gem from certain angles there was a royal purple hue that would emanate from the stone. I laid a hand on the mountain's face, and when I did I could feel serenity as a soothing stream flowing into me. How I felt when I stood upon the onyx mountain was entirely different from how I now felt. On the onyx mountain, urgency filled me to pray and curiosity led me into the mystery of God. Here I felt at complete rest. I could feel an overwhelming increase of peace. Holy Spirit held a look of Godly pride upon His face toward me. I could tell that He was excited to share such an experience with me.

"How did we get here so quickly Holy Spirit?" I asked amazed.

"We transported here," Holy Spirit said. "There is no distance in the spirit. In Heaven you can go from here to there in the blink of an eye, so long as you have faith of course."

With the shimmering diamond beneath my feet, Holy Spirit and I walked over to the mountain's edge.

Because of the stone's purity it felt as though I was hiking in mid-winter, scaling a snow covered mountain. Looking over the ledge I could see parts of Heaven that were thousands of feet below us. I could see the splendorous garden as well. Peering at the Tree of Life's golden leaves even from this height still impacted me. The sight filled me with passion and a sense of purpose. Far away, yet still in the garden, was what looked like an enormous mansion. It was made from the purest of marble and granite, easily larger than a well-established city.

"That is the Father's house," Holy Spirit said. "That is where the Hall of Mantles and many other great places are."

As I looked upon the impressive piece of architecture, my feet kept me moving along the mountainous floor. The cliff that we walked upon had about a 15 foot width to it, yet as we continued forward the cliff began to narrow. We ventured ahead as the cliff shrunk to about a three foot width. With our backs to the mountain and our chests to the sky, Holy Spirit and I shuffled along the diamond path. I had seen this very thing happen in movies where action stars would trail upon small cliffs. My heart would pound as I watched anticipating a fall. Yet for me, this experience was completely different. As I breathed in the air of Heaven, I was breathing in peace itself. Fear actually could not exist in me. I just walked in a state of awe, unswervingly focused on Heaven's beauty.

Looking over to Holy Spirit I felt a wonderful sense of assurance. I was on an adventure with my best of friends. Knowing His true identity made this moment just that much more special. I could be in any circumstance and be at peace if He were with me.

As we approached a corner on the mountain, white flakes drifted on wind currents from the other

The Creator's Heart

side. When what I at first thought was snow hit my face, I was surprised that the flakes were not at all cold, nor did they melt. The flakes were as hard as rock.

In that instant I had to make a decision. Should I continue gazing at the granite house? Or should I follow my curiosity to discover the mysterious flakes' source? I looked to Holy Spirit for the answer, yet the expression on His face gave me no direction. He just stared at me, waiting for me to choose what to do. I remembered what Holy Spirit told me when we were in the small garden about times of mandate and invitation. This was one of those times of invitation. Looking back to the mighty mansion one last time, I swore to myself that I would soon visit it. A hunger for adventure swept me further along the trail, closer to the mountain's corner.

As I neared closer to the diamond corner, I could hear tapping that resounded in groups of three.

Tap tap tap. Tap tap tap.

Rounding the corner, the path opened up to an expansive ledge. Shimmering flakes flew in every direction as though there was a blizzard occurring upon the diamond mountain. From where the flakes flew stood a stunning sight. Beneath an intricate hammer and chisel hard at work, was a 40 foot tall statue being constructed. The statue was not made from marble. It was being sculpted right out of the diamond mountain itself. As the artist tapped away at the masterpiece with his hammer and chisel, it was plainly known to me who the man was; however, I will choose to leave his identity hidden.

As I brushed some of the flakes that rested upon the diamond floor with my foot, the artist suddenly stopped his sculpting in mid swing and began descending his ladder. Reaching the ladder's base, I saw that he was a short man. He had long, frazzled hair and an unruly beard. Diamond flakes covered his face, hair and beard. Diamond dust covered almost every inch of his skin. He resembled what I would assume one of the Old Testament prophets would have looked like. With a hammer in one hand and a chisel in the other, the sculptor stood before me with his masterpiece towering behind him. It was a sight that any art historian would have loved to see. A master standing before his soon to be finished work.

Being an artist myself, it was an unbelievable privilege to be with the artist who I admire most, other than the Creator Himself. Speaking excitedly, the man said, "You are the first to come to see the sculpture I am sculpting. It is a beautiful sight, is it not? It is quite something to be sculpting a statue out of diamond instead of marble."

"I can only imagine," I said in response. Holy Spirit was standing off to the side watching the master artist and I speak. "Why is it that you decided to sculpt this particular piece?" I asked.

Before responding, the master sculptor studied me for a moment. His intense gaze was by no means intimidating. His gaze was full of thought, as though he was deciding how to lay out the answer to my question. As he pondered, I saw a greatness in the man. In this saint was a garden of understanding. He was one who honoured mystery as the adventure that it was.

"I chose this sculpture for two reasons. One reason is because it symbolizes a revelation of humankind's true worth. Secondly, because this particular image symbolizes the arts."

The man continued, "A while back I was worshipping the Almighty in the throne room with many other saints, when the Son of Man stepped down from His throne. He walked over to me with a requested mandate. He asked me to build a monument that would be a sign of remembrance for all of eternity. It was to be a statue that would mark the revival that will be taking place. In Heaven there are many different objects that function as monuments. These monuments mark different times when God moved in a history changing way. Not only do they carry the memory of events, but they carry the experience of such events. They carry the anointing that was prevalent in that time. To look upon them is to experience the same anointing which flowed from Heaven in that time. This statue will be one of these markers."

I looked back up to the mighty statue in a new state of awe.

"While I dwelled on Earth I sculpted this same piece. However, this of course is much larger and is being sculpted from a pricier stone. When I first chiseled this on Earth, I wanted to create a statue that showed the beauty of humankind. I wanted to present an image that reflected the likeness of God, so that those who looked upon my work would understand their own importance and greatness. For far too long, those in the church have willingly remained in their insecurities due to a humility that is false. You already know this, but this movement taking place is a saint's movement. The saints are waking up to understand their worth."

The artist pointed to the sculpture and explained, "Every time people look upon this statue, they will remember when the multitudes woke up to their true identity. You are living in a time when history will be changed forever in a very dramatic way."

"This statue also marks a new move of renaissance that is now taking place. The Bride of Christ is about to encounter the Creator's heart to a depth that she never has before. When she encounters the Creator, she will walk in a spirit of creativity. Back in the early

Renaissance in the 1400's to 1600's much of the church rejected the arts. Many who called themselves prophets would construct raids to destroy art in the name of our Lord. Beauty was seen as vile. Creativity was seen as lewd because the religious feared change and feared losing control. Ah, but it was a beautiful time. In that time humankind learned how to express what they experienced in the inner man. Some of the greatest art in all of history was thought up and brought to life in that time. Since the church rejected the arts, in many ways the Bride handed her anointing for creativity over to the world."

"The same happened in the 1960's. There was a release of a fresh sound of music, yet the church branded it as demonic. Therefore, instead of the church embracing God's move of new sound, they handed the anointing for creativity over to the world. So much has been lost, yet there is so much that upcoming generations will restore in the name of the Creator."

Holy Spirit placed a hand upon my shoulder and He began to speak, "Understanding is only an encounter away, Nameless One. And that which you behold, you become. Just as I had brought you to the Mountain of Intercession to receive a burden for revival, I have brought you to this Mountain of Creativity that you might understand the Creator's heart."

Out from His robe, He pulled forth a small diamond flask. Inside held sparkling-blue water. "This is water fetched from this mountain's River of Revelation. Take a drink, Nameless One."

As I brought the flask to my lips and swallowed the water, Holy Spirit laid a graceful hand upon my head. Almost immediately visions started to flood my sight. The visions began so subtly that I almost had to intentionally focus in order to see them. Then the intensity of them began increasing until I saw the vision plainly. What I saw was not at all what I had expected. I began to see the creation account unfolding. Yet it unfolded in a way that surprised me. It was not as black and white as I had heard or read about in the past. The creation account was the by-product of the deepest form of intimacy and desire. Seeing creation unfold may have been the most intimate thing I have ever witnessed. I will try my best to describe it.

I saw three sitting together as a Trinity of love. Father, Son and Holy Spirit communed. They laughed together in joyous celebration. To see the three of them together as One was a sight to not soon be forgotten. They were completely unified in relationship, never lacking intimacy or vulnerability. When out of the Trinity's laughter birthed a thought. That thought was to create humankind, who would be an extension of the Trinity's family. At that very moment a swell of emotion filled the atmosphere around them. That emotion was a wild love. A love so passionate that it stirred the Trinity to action, invoking the aspect of them that was the Creator.

Together as One, the Trinity spoke the Earth's form into shape. They sung in a three chord harmony and Heaven's figure was fashioned. As sovereign poetry escaped their lips, Light rested upon the Earth and held it in an embrace. Light whispered to the Earth a song of comfort, promising that its glory would cover the Earth's body in whole one day. In a triumphant shout, the Trinity's call split the waters in two. Divided, they were no longer known as one, but both sky and sea received their individual names.

In a deep rumbling voice, the Trinity called forth Land to rise to the ocean's surface. Thus the land and waters were separate. The Trinity then whispered poetry into the soil of the land, calling awake grass, herbs, and various species of trees. All arose from their slumber. The sky welcomed the awakened sleepers, promising to water them with the gift of dew. In excitement the Trinity shouted like a trumpet. In that single word, the sun and moon were created. Stars now filled the Heavens. The mighty sun smiled down upon the Earth promising to bless it with heat and nourishment. The sun then sat upon his throne to rule over the day. The moon in turn sat upon her throne to rule over the night. As husband and wife they watched the Earth, and from their reign birthed a child whose name was time. Time vowed to keep the Earth in check and balance. To do so, Time gave Earth a variety of gifts. Those gifts were seconds, days, seasons, years, centuries and millenniums.

Seeing that both sky and sea were empty of life, the Trinity spoke, and by one word they were filled with creatures that flew and swam. By a second word the land was filled with beasts that crawled and ran. The variety of animals between those of the sky, sea and land were innumerable. Their very existence was a promise that it would take until the end of Earth's long life to discover the mystery of their diversity.

It was now time to create the very thing that was the catalyst of why creation began in the first place. As Three who were unified in every thought and emotion, the Trinity spoke as One and said, "Let Us make humankind in Our image."

Before the Trinity spoke forth humankind, they waited in silence for only a moment. This moment was not a moment of hesitancy. They reveled in this place because they knew that by the sound of one word from their lips, the greatest love story ever composed would begin to be written. Once the moment passed, the Trinity began to sing. They sang a song so wonderful that all of Heaven and Earth stopped and listened. The Son of Man started the song by singing a single word. In the tone of a baritone, the song echoed throughout all of creation and began a birthing. Submitting to the song's rhythm, bone and marrow spun together in an obedient dance, molding one shape, and then another. Muscle and flesh dressed the forms customizing each. First the masculine and then the feminine. When the bodies were complete, in a bass voice the Father then sung a word. At the sound of His voice, something awoke within the man and woman. That which came to life in them was the need to love and to be loved. The once lifeless faces were now filled with emotion and personality. Lastly, as a tenor, Holy Spirit sung a word in the purest falsetto creation had ever heard. And in that moment both man and woman were filled with the breath of life. All of the Heavens and Earth marveled in awe. The oceans were still and the wind was steady. Grass, plants and trees held their breath speechless. The sun and moon gaped in wonder. Every animal listened soundlessly, conscious to not miss even a single note from the timeless song. For in that day, fashioned from a wild love came forth a son and daughter.

Renaissance Restored

When the vision of creation fell from my eyes, I found myself on hands and knees upon the diamond floor. Before, when I had contemplated the creation account, I had always marveled at the raw power of God. Yet now the story took on a deeper meaning for me. The creation account was a story about God's deep desire for His children. The entire reason that the world was created was so that the Father could find His children on Earth.

My life was fashioned because of the Trinity's love for me, I thought.

After a time, Holy Spirit helped me up. I had completely forgotten that Holy Spirit and the artist were with me. I looked up at them, feeling disoriented, much like how I felt when I drank from the onyx mountain's river. Even though I wanted more time to meditate on what I just saw, the artist continued to speak of what God was doing in the arts. I had to lay pondering my personal revelation aside for the moment, to catch the message that this prophetic mouthpiece had for the church.

"What you just saw is what unlocks creativity," the expert sculptor said. "True art is birthed through experience. Art is not only something that should be appealing to the eye, or a simple production of excellence. It is to be a manifestation of one's soul and spirit. If an artist is moved by a specific sunrise, he will try to capture that moment on canvas. Art preserves an encounter for others to experience. An artist's job is to use art as a sign post for their experience. Therefore, whoever looks upon it will experience what the artist experienced when they were first inspired. Art is an open heaven. It is an invitation into the soul and spirit of the one who created it. Understand that I am not only referring to painting. I am referring to any creative medium, whether that be music, writing, painting, architecture; you name it. Humankind was God's masterpiece because our existence is not only a manifestation of God's masterful craftsmanship. It was God's encounter with a wild love for His children that moved Him to create. Now every son and daughter of God is a signpost for the world to encounter God's wild love, which first inspired Him to create His masterpiece."

The master artist continued, "As this generation and generations to come fall deeper in love with the Creator, the arts will be used as one of the most powerful ways to reach people, because the church will paint, draw, play instruments, sing and write out of their encounters with God, permitting others to experience the same."

As the man spoke it felt as though I was receiving an impartation on behalf of the body of Christ. It felt like streams of paint were coursing through my veins. New realms of creativity were opening. My imagination was broadening.

Holy Spirit entered into the conversation again. "I tell you the truth, Nameless One, this sculpture has slept for over 500 years on Earth. However the revelation from which it was created, an understanding of humankind's significance is about to shine throughout the nations. The revelation from which this sculpture was created is about to awaken. Stone will become flesh. And the mighty mountain will sing poems that will heal the broken hearted. It will sing poems that only rivers can pronounce. Art is about to be used by the church as a tool to awaken identity."

Something then caught my eye in my peripheral vision. Whirling through the sky was what looked like a shimmering blue phoenix. The large yet elegant creature landed upon the diamond's ledge. Standing beside the artist and Holy Spirit, I watched the divine being. Even though this creature looked almost dragon-like, I knew in my spirit that it was actually an angel. Since this angel had more of a feminine demeanor, I will refer to it as a 'she'. This angel stood at about 12 feet tall, yet her wing span must have reached at least 20 feet. The angel glowed in a brilliant-blue flame.

"This is a very high ranked angel. This angel's name is *Wisdom*," Holy Spirit said. "I have called her here to carry us to different places where you need to go to inherit revelation. As we ride with this angel, you will receive an impartation from what she is called to minister."

The angel stood gracefully before us. She bore eyes that were both sophisticated and radiant. They were set in her face resembling light blue topaz gemstones. Even though I was quite enthralled with the idea of flying with such a creature, a question lingered in my mind.

"If we need to leave here, then why not just transport like we did when we came to this mountain? Why do we need to take the time to fly?"

Before Holy Spirit could answer, Wisdom piped up. "Because, Nameless One, what you learn during the journey is more important than what you learn at your journey's end." The angel's voice was so elegant that when she spoke, my inner core felt soothed. Her tone was what I assumed an angel's tone should sound like. Heavenly.

Wisdom continued, "The reason why the lessons you learn on your journey are more important is because they train you to hold onto the promise of your destiny. One who fails to heed the lessons of day to day life will never steward the promises of tomorrow."

Wisdom's words felt as though they carried tremendous weight to them. I knew in my spirit that the insight she gave would be a beacon that would lead me into further realms of understanding. "This is why Holy Spirit has called me here. I am hunting you, because at present, your zeal is destructive because it is not yet wielded by wisdom."

Holy Spirit then began validating Wisdom's ministry. "The Son of Man often commissions Wisdom to walk alongside of different leaders in the body of Christ throughout the Earth. Many moves of God have been sustained with longevity because of the message she carries."

When I looked back to the angel, she was now kneeling down on one knee. Wisdom then spoke reverently. "It is my greatest honour to serve one of the royal ambassadors of Heaven."

Wisdom then turned around with her back towards us, waiting for Holy Spirit and me to climb aboard. Considering Wisdom's size, I never once felt concern as to whether she could carry Holy Spirit and me or not. However, before I mounted Wisdom's back, I turned to the artist and thanked him for the unforgettable experience and impartation he had given to me. Wearing a look that showed he was sincerely honoured to do so, he nodded his head, turned around and ascended back up his ladder to continue his work. Holy Spirit and I approached the angel and climbed onto her back. Mounted upon Wisdom, the angel leaped off of the diamond platform to catch the first gust of wind.

I turned back, and waved to say farewell to the great creator. The man waved back and shouted to me a final revelation, "Remember, Nameless One! Never fear thinking in a different way than others think. It is in this place of courage where Heaven's originality is expressed!"

As we drifted away, I listened to the light tap that resounded in groups of three until it was out of ear's reach.

Illuminated By Wisdom

Into the distant skies we soared. Although we were flying in the direction of the Father's house, I knew in my spirit that we were not in fact going there. After taking a steady course for a time, Wisdom took a sharp left turn. We were flying to a destination to the far left of the mansion. Flying atop of Wisdom felt much different than when I flew upon Holy Spirit's back when He was in the form of an eagle. On Holy Spirit's back there was an undeniable strength, whereas flying with Wisdom felt more delicate, as though I were riding upon a giant stork.

As we flew, Holy Spirit began to speak, "What you have experienced in this adventure up until this point has been the Inner Court of the Third Heaven. Every mountain you saw, the Garden of Intimacy, and even the private garden where you discovered my true identity were part of the Inner Court. Where we are now going is Heaven's Outer Court."

Even though time functioned differently in Heaven than it did on Earth, it felt as though the Outer Court of Heaven was quite a distance away from the diamond mountain in the Inner Court. Wisdom utilized the time it took to travel as an opportunity to teach.

With a graceful yet authoritative voice, the angel spoke, "I have walked alongside many great leaders, Nameless One. I have co-labored and given counsel to some of the greatest of God's generals that have ever walked the Earth. I have at times given very intricate instruction and counsel for city transformation. Where most leaders could excel in the meticulous, many failed in the simple. If I could speak one word of wisdom into you alone concerning how to be a great leader, it would be Matthew 22:37-39."

Wisdom then began quoting the verses, "Love the Lord your God with all your heart, with all your soul, and with all your mind. Secondly, love your neighbor as yourself."

As Wisdom spoke, it felt as though new realms of revelation were being opened to me. Even though her tone was soft, how she spoke was not overly pastoral. This angel's ministry to humankind was not to tend to the brokenhearted. As a teacher of both wisdom and revelation she spoke rather sternly, confirming to me that in that moment I was her pupil and that I needed to be more than attentive.

Wisdom continued, "Every truth comes out of these two commandments. If you can do these two things well, then it is nearly impossible for you not to see sustained revival. Saturate yourself in intimacy with the Lord. Do not encounter love as a concept, encounter Love as a person. Allow yourself to be so infatuated with God, where you cannot help but to experience Him in every facet of your life; in your heart, soul, mind, relationships, finances, everything. Never step out of the secret place. Never isolate aspects of your identity from Him. Receive Him in full, that you may be whole. As you embrace wholeness through intimacy, you invite the Son of God to be formed and fashioned within every aspect of who you are. Abide under the shelter of God's wings. This is the safe place and the abode of grace. Every fall-out in ministry comes out of not doing this first commandment well. Allow no disconnects between yourself and the Godhead."

"Loving God is the first step that you must take in order to love others. The second step is learning to love yourself. Encountering God in the secret place will empower you to love yourself. If God's commandment is to love your neighbor as you love yourself, then we see that how much you choose to love yourself is the standard of how much you can authentically love others. You cannot truly give away the love of God if you do not know how to receive it yourself. You are to freely give as you have freely received. You must learn to embrace yourself for who God has created you to be. This increases the capacity to love others because your love for yourself is great. To love others is one of the most Godly characteristics you can possibly obtain. Those who will be seated in high places in Heaven are those who have truly learned to love."

"As you make the decision to love, you step into increase concerning how to receive the love of God through others. Many men and women have had great falls in their ministries because of a lack of trust and accountability in relationships. The church is a family. Learn to view them as such. When you do, the connections you make while ministering are not simply connections, they are a lineage being reunited. This is what will make the nations wonder in awe, not an impressive man-made network of people. With family surrounding you who truly know and see you, it is nearly impossible to fail."

I could feel Wisdom's words marking my heart. I began to pray internally. *Lord, teach me how to live my life from these two commandments. Help me to continue to fall deeply in love with both You and people.*

Wisdom continued her teaching, "You are living in great times of acceleration, Nameless One. There are seasons of sowing and seasons of reaping. However, this is a time where God is doing things at such an increased speed that you can scatter a seed with your left hand and pick the fruit with your right simultaneously. Where 100 years ago it may have taken an individual an entire lifetime to grasp a specific truth, people in this time will understand that same truth in a moment."

"In order for the church to steward everything that God is doing on the Earth today well, there needs to be an increase of wisdom. It is important to understand that with the more impressive gifts such as words of knowledge and gifts of healing, you can draw the eyes of the nations. However, only with wisdom can you steward those nations. Because of this there is about to be a drastic increase of the wisdom of the Lord in this time throughout the Earth."

"In order to truly fathom wisdom, we must understand the fear of the Lord, since it is in fact the beginning of wisdom. People have viewed the fear of the Lord through an unhealthy lens for millenniums. Many have feared the Lord, deeming Him as distant and unapproachable; when really, to walk in a fear of the Lord means to hate evil (Proverbs 8:13)."

"We are to hate evil because God hates evil. He does not hate evil and sin because He simply disagrees with it in principle. God hates evil and sin because they hurt His children. Every truth is rooted in the heart of God. In order to come to the beginning of wisdom, you must understand His heart. You must understand His will."

"God's will is that His children would not experience evil, but that they would have an endless encounter with goodness. His will is that the culture of Heaven would invade Earth. This is the beginning of wisdom."

At that statement I shut my eyes and soaked in its satisfying depth. As Wisdom talked on, I could feel Heaven's outer court drawing nearer. It was a refreshing excursion. The wind through which we travelled stroked my face and Wisdom's words caressed my understanding. Onwards we flew until we were at the very brink of Heaven.

Heaven's Many Courts

Considering Heaven's enormity, the thought had never even crossed my mind that it might have an end. We landed on the inside of Heaven's gate, which was made of one giant pearl. The gate stood about 30 feet tall in height and as far as I could see was endless as I looked at it from left to right. The gate wore a pink and silvery aura around it. From the gate trailed a street made completely of translucent gold that led deep into Heaven, back in the direction from which we had come. Not a single person or angel was in sight other than Wisdom, Holy Spirit and me. The Outer Court felt much different than the Inner Court. The atmosphere in the Inner Court was saturated in intimacy, where the Outer Court had much more of a militant feel to it. Yet, in both places of Heaven, love was still triumphant.

I was suddenly struck by a spark of desire. I had a sudden interest to see what resided on the other side of the wall. Without thinking twice I gripped the pearly wall and began to climb. As I climbed, Holy Spirit began to climb up behind me. I had hoped that Wisdom would come up with us; however, she stayed on the ground awaiting our return.

A Timeless Journey

When Holy Spirit and I reached the top, we sat upon the wall, gaping at the view before us. From atop the pearly gate I could see warrior angels stationed on the opposite side of the wall. With their backs to the gate and their chests to what laid before them, the angels stood mightily, as unshakable as stone. Thousands upon thousands of angels stood upon a cloudy floor, geared for battle in a straight line before the gate. Each wore shimmering armor from head to toe made from a metal I had never seen up until this point. The metal was not steel, iron, silver or gold. I knew that it was a metal that could not be found on Earth. Each angel held a broadsword singlehandedly into the air, never flinching even once. Every sword that pointed to the sky was clothed in a fire that danced upon shining blades. As fire licked the swords, each one resembled a torch held high, offering itself as a guide to those who desired to come to this wonderful place. The angels stood tirelessly, just as I knew they had for thousands of years before that moment. They were an impenetrable shield to guard Heaven at all times.

Beyond the pearly gates, and far past the warrior angels, was a sight that baffled me. It was Earth. Yet it was not Earth as we know and see it. It was what Earth looked like from Heaven's perspective. I could see what Earth looked like in the natural realm and the spiritual realm simultaneously. Although I was only sitting in one place, I could view the Earth from every angle. It was as though my sight could zoom in and out. If I chose, I could watch the Earth as a whole from a distance as though peering at it from outer space. Yet I could also target my sight in on every country, city, community and individual. Both the intricacy and breadth of Earth could be seen in totality.

It was fascinating what was taking place on Earth. There were regions in the Earth where the glory of the Lord glowed brightly, and others that appeared more dimmed. However, even though some regions were dimmer, the glory of the Lord was still present there; it was just veiled. Where some of the regions were darkened, demonic principalities rested there warring for those specific regions. The principalities all looked different. Most resembled some form of animal. In the regions that shone brightly, angelic principalities were stationed.

I narrowed my sight in on a specific city that had a demonic principality over it. This principality looked like an enormous bear skin rug that draped over the entire city. Its fur was a dark grey. The principality bared fierce teeth and had a look of hatred and greed in its eyes. Below the principality were different demonic ranks. *Powers* that governed different quadrants of the city and oversaw different men and women who held great influence were in place under the principality. The powers looked like kings and queens who were deformed in one way or another. Each was dressed as though they were royalty, yet instead of carrying a demeanor of love and nobility, each was filled with anger and malice. Each power carried a staff, which was a symbol to show the false authority that they had in the city.

Beneath the powers were *rulers* who oversaw different communities. The rulers looked like 10 foot-long-black tigers. However, their faces resembled the faces of men. Out of their backs were large wings that were similar to a bat's wings. The muscled cats would prowl around trying to keep those below them in rank in check and order. Much lesser ranked demons were in place below the rulers. These demons came in all shapes and forms. Some resembled men. Some looked more like goblins or trolls, and others looked like different animals.

The demonic structure was highly militant, yet extremely disorganized. Demons roamed the streets mostly in packs. There were entire groups that consisted of demons of jealousy, and other groups which contained demons of anger. Some packs had demons of lust. All went throughout the city with the purpose of placing people in bondage. Even though there were specific demonic authorities set in place over this city, the demons lacked greatly in submission. This is why there was such disorganization. They lacked in submission because they were slaves themselves to the same bondages that they tried to enslave others in. The demons of jealousy were continuously jealous of one another, especially towards those who were in higher ranks than themselves and the demons of anger were constantly fighting amongst one another.

I then began seeing Christians walking throughout the city. Many wore the same false breastplates of righteousness that had been worn in the Garden of Intimacy. Most of those Christians walked around sluggishly, oblivious to what was going on around them in the spirit realm. Some of the demons would often come and strike one of the Christians, yet they would do nothing in return. They just went about their lives in apathy and passivity. Every one of them that wore the false breastplates had at least one demon following them everywhere they went. Since there were specific demons appointed to influential leaders in the city, there were entire businesses and schools that were trapped in bondage.

"Where are all of the angels, Holy Spirit?" I asked.

"Every single person, church, city and nation has angels that are specifically appointed to them," Holy Spirit said. "However, much of the church does not understand that they are called to co-labour with the angelic through prayer and declaration. When the saints pray and prophesy, it actually releases the angelic to wage war on the enemy. The prophet Daniel understood this greatly. In Daniel 10, when the principality of Persia held an angel captive who possessed a message for

Daniel, Daniel fasted for 21 days, which enabled the archangel Michael to free the angel that was captive. It was something that Daniel did in the natural realm that empowered the angelic in the spiritual realm. So really, the angels are waiting for the church to stand for their city. Once they do, there will be a drastic change in the city's spiritual climate."

I then saw a few Christians who wore the true breastplates of righteousness. In the dark atmosphere around them, the light that shone from them radiated far and wide. Numerous angels gathered around these particular saints. Coming from each of the true breastplate bearers shot a beam of light straight into the sky, piercing through the principality's back. The principality seemed to be in great pain because of this. Beams of light were shooting out from its back in various places. It was interesting to see that these Christians' very existence was a hindrance to the principality. These saints began walking up to the Christians who were in bondage. The saints who wore the true breastplates would then lay a hand on the false breastplate bearers' chests and would begin to pray and declare life into them. As they did, the same lightning that I had seen earlier shooting from the Tree of Life would shoot from their hands, shattering the leather garments. The now freed Christians would then begin to project a light that would shoot into the air and through the principality.

As this would happen, the principality would shout in a wild roar. Angels began rushing around the Christians as they experienced freedom. The Christians began walking throughout the city as one. Their light shone forth and woke up unbelievers from their sleep. As they awoke, the unbelievers could not deny the light that they saw and joined the group of believers. What was once a myriad of individual beams piercing through the back of the principality now became one unified beam as the saints rallied together.

The beam shone brilliantly. It shone so bright that it completely burned away the principality from its throne over the city. Now when one looked into the sky, instead of seeing darkness, you could see directly into Heaven. Over the city was now an open Heaven. All powers and rulers lost grip of their false authority and ceased to have any form of reign. Darkness that once ruled was gone, and shadow was no more. The saints then resounded in a shout of praise and worship. As they did so, what looked like a giant-silver dove descended from Heaven to fill the throne that the evil principality left void. This dove was the angelic principality that would minister to the city.

When the angelic principality took charge, each district in the city began to understand its destiny to steward citywide revival. Each community became a safe place of family for the broken and lonely. People with profound influence in business and government began serving the Lord with great diligence. No one who came in the vicinity of this city was untouched by the presence of the Lord. Some would simply come in contact with the land and be healed of sickness and disease. Others would be delivered from addictions.

As the dove rested over the city, I could see giant doors that hung in the sky. These doors began to open for the first time in centuries. This city was ordained to be a resource to the world, and these doors were the doors to the nations. I then saw a few people who were specifically chosen by God ascend into the sky and fly through the doors. These saints went to other cities and nations training different regions how to sustain a citywide movement.

Holy Spirit's eyes twinkled as He watched the glorious sight. With passion in His voice, He asked, "Tell me, Nameless One, do you believe that a nation can be born again in a day?"

I waited a moment letting the question linger in the air. "Of course. It is what I live for," I finally responded confidently.

A smile spread over Holy Spirit's face. "Many people can dream big dreams. However, in order for change to occur it requires us to wake up and make our dreams a reality. Often people refuse to wake up and take action because they fear the possibility of failure or disappointment. But, I tell you the truth, a time is coming where the world will see this very thing. Entire cities, entire nations being born again in a day. The kingdoms of this world have become the kingdoms of the Son of Man, Jesus. He shall reign forever and ever. Many only have the faith to see 100 souls come into the kingdom. Others have the faith for thousands. But I tell you the truth, in this day, I am training the church to believe for billions."

"Take note as to why this change began to occur, Nameless One. What you just saw were believers in this city recognizing who they were, and doing something with that. It started with an internal revelation and progressed into an outward manifestation. These believers needed to come to the revelation that they in fact did not abide under the power of the demonic principality over this city. They rest and abide over it, in the Heavens in Christ. They are the dominant force and authority in that city. Once that understanding took shape, it was nearly impossible for change not to occur."

I looked forth once again to watch the Earth. I began to see this citywide revival impacting regions surrounding it. The revival then spread forth to a nation. Then two. Then many.

"The whole Earth will be filled with His glory," I whispered.

A Timeless Journey

Different places on Earth began to carry the same atmosphere of love that I had been experiencing my whole time while in Heaven. My heart leaped with joy as sickness ceased to exist in specific regions. I laughed when the masses were encountering the heart of God. Sons and daughters across the world worshipped the one true God; Father, Son and Holy Spirit.

Holy Spirit and I began our descent down the pearly gate. As we travelled downward, only one thought filled my mind. *Nations born again in a day.* I ran the thought over and over again in my mind. Much of the church has trouble believing for even 100 souls to be born into the Kingdom of Heaven, when God was believing for the salvation of entire nations.

Reaching the bottom, Wisdom was kneeling on one knee again, facing the opposite direction of us. With no hesitation we climbed the divine being and took flight once again.

Knowledge, Wisdom and Revelation

After silence lingered for a time during our flight, Holy Spirit finally broke the stillness by asking me a question. "How come you haven't asked me where we are going yet, Nameless One? Usually you ask more questions then are even necessary."

I smirked, knowing that Holy Spirit was trying to tease me. "I haven't asked because I already know where we are going."

"Do you now?" Holy Spirit said knowingly.

"Yes," I said. "We are going to the Father's house."

"You are beginning to understand my leading better and better each moment, Nameless One. It is an important revelation to know that you and I are one, just as I am one with the Father and the Son. The sons and daughters of God are the extension of the Trinity's family."

The marble mansion grew closer. I could sense it. As we flew onward, I felt an instant shift in the atmosphere as we crossed from the Outer Court back into Heaven's Inner Court. It was like an instant aroma of grace being poured over me. We voyaged through the sky until our destination was in plain sight.

Much quicker than I assumed, the house stood before us. As I looked upon the marble homestead, I could hardly comprehend its enormity. Yet, as enormous as it was, the detail on the house was pristine. Intricate carvings marked every inch of each wall. Banners of every colour danced in the wind, some larger than regular sized houses. When I had seen castles in the past, usually a daunting and lonely feeling would accompany them. Yet this house was fully inviting. It was in fact lively. The halls and rooms of this house were full of laughter and joy. This was a house where the family of God could be together. Angels and saints were everywhere to be seen. Many walked around the outskirts of the house in the numerous gardens that surrounded it. Animals that on Earth would be deemed as wild and dangerous hung around in the gardens, for here they were tame and harmless. Children played in the garden streams gleefully, never once fearing the animals that were near them. In fact I could see some of the children playing with the animals. There was something precious about seeing an animal such as a mighty lion playing so tenderly with a small child.

There were several outdoor halls that were occupied by both angels and saints. There were also numerous outdoor meeting places where many would worship in song and dance. Suspended above the mansion was a rainbow. Yet this rainbow was so luminous that it looked as though it was made up from every single rainbow that has been displayed on the

Earth since Noah's time. The rainbow would often rain colorful gem stones upon the saints, angels and animals. I knew that this was a place where not a single promise went unfulfilled. Even though there is often a negative connotation to this word, the only word I can think of to describe this magnificent place would be that it was *magical*.

     Swirling downwards in a steady spiral, Wisdom's feet met the ground. We landed directly in front of one of the house's many entrances. Since we landed on a rather high entrance point, I walked over to one of the house's ledges and looked over to see multitudes of people who made this place their home. Upon flawless marble ledges, saints and angels stood with one another conversing. Throughout some of the outside hallways, others travelled to new destinations in the castle. Leading up to the entrance were hundreds of feet of twisting and turning stairs that were carved directly out of the marble walls. This marble staircase was packed with saints and angels who were journeying up the colossal house. I was beginning to realize that this mansion was in fact once a mountain, and in whole was carved into this home. A busy home at that.

    My eyes then began wandering upwards. Even though this specific entrance was suspended many feet into the air, my sight still scaled the mountainous walls ever high-ward. The enormity of this house was even more overwhelming close up than it was from far away. When my eyes reached the end of the towering walls, I peered at the gleaming rainbow that draped over the house like a banner of love. As I gazed into the rainbow it felt as though there was an ocean of hope pouring directly into me.

    Suddenly every saint and angel at the house stopped what they were doing and sang forth a song of victory. With the rainbow hanging over me, and innumerable saints and angels singing around me, I was taken in by the moment. A song flooded my mind that I did not know before that time. I began to sing with the saints wholeheartedly:

> *"Father, Son and Spirit, One;*
> *A Trinity of unity.*
> *Communing deep with daughters and sons,*
> *Extending Heaven's family."*
>
> *"I am not alone, I am not alone.*
> *Is the children's eternal melody.*
> *I belong, I belong,*
> *is our endless song of testimony."*

Once the song was finished, everyone continued with whatever it was they had been doing, whether that was talking amongst one another, walking, or playing with the animals in the gardens. However, the worship in their hearts did not stop. It never stopped. In this place I could tell that every saint was directly linked to the heart of God at all times. That was one of the blessings of ascension; eternal awareness of intimacy with the Godhead.

I looked back behind me to the entrance where Wisdom brought me. The doors of the entrance were at least 25 feet tall and were the colour of a deep scarlet. Out of the marble walls framing the red doors budded flowers of all sorts. I grabbed one of the doors' solid gold handles and gave it a tug. As the door swung wide, I was greeted by a wonderful sight. Before me was a room that dwarfed any room that I have ever laid my eyes upon. In this place, books upon books were piled on top of one another. Scrolls upon scrolls. Endless bookshelves filled different aisles. There were countless corridors leading to different sections that were just as colossal as the room I was now peering into. The number of books in this place was countless. In fact, it

Knowledge, Wisdom and Revelation

seemed as though the entire world itself could not contain as many books as were laid out before my eyes. Some of the books looked new. Others looked old, yet did not give the appearance of being fragile in the slightest. Many people were there studying the vast variety of books and scrolls. Some had hundreds of books stacked around them all at once. This place was a treasury of revelation, all at my hand's grasp. Heaven's library was only a few steps away.

As Holy Spirit, Wisdom and I all stepped into the library, Holy Spirit began leading me to different sections and aisles.

Running His hand over different books, Holy Spirit said, "These books carry great significance you know. Every move of God that has ever taken place throughout the entire course of history is recorded in these books. Look at this one for instance."

Holy Spirit grabbed a book that was royal red with gold trim around it from one of the bookshelves. "This book holds numerous testimonies that occurred in John G. Lake's ministry."

As Holy Spirit handed me the book, I was surprised by its significant weight. I slowly opened the book to a random page, and as I did the very anointing that rested upon John G. Lake's life began to envelope me. As I read the different testimonies, I could hardly stand because the power of the Lord was coming upon me so strongly. I could feel a passion for the sick and inflicted stirring within me as I never had before.

After sitting under this anointing for a time, I closed up the book. "Why did I just come under that anointing, Holy Spirit?" I asked.

A Timeless Journey

"You felt the anointing because these books do not only hold stories, they also carry the experiences behind the stories," Holy Spirit answered.

Wisdom then began answering my question alongside of Holy Spirit, but with a teaching. "This library is the place where knowledge, wisdom and revelation meet. Some ministries only place value in one of the three, disabling their ministry from walking in wholeness concerning understanding. Those who only value knowledge miss experience and proper application for knowledge. Those who value only revelation risk arrogance and over spiritualism. And those who only value wisdom succumb to following their own intellect instead of being led through their experience with the Lord. Knowledge, wisdom and revelation are supposed to function together as a trinity of understanding. If you separate them from one another, then you are leaving empty seats for ignorance to fill."

Wisdom carried on with her exhortation. "Knowledge, wisdom and revelation are the keys to authentic intellectualism. People too often assume that Old Testament prophets must have been so over spiritual that they were borderline un-relatable to their present times; when in fact some of the Old Testament prophets were the most profound of intellectuals. They did not just sit around having prophetic encounters, only valuing revelation. They had a true hunger for knowledge. Since there were no such things as the internet or printing companies back then, when prophets would want to know something about history, they would actually have to seek out that knowledge. The prophets would at times travel great distances to find even a single book. The prophets had the ears of kings to speak to. So, not only did they seek knowledge and revelation, but they would allow wisdom to wield both. It was because they valued knowledge, wisdom and revelation that the Lord could entrust them to instruct entire nations."

"Be a meeting place for this trinity to marry, and the deep wells of understanding will be available to you."

Holding the royal red book in both hands, I looked at it in wonder.

As I was lost in my inner thoughts, a sound filled the silence that stole my attention. The sound was a saintly voice that echoed through one of the corridors. A huge part of me did not want to leave this first section of the library, yet the voice that I heard held an irresistible authority. Even if I took to examining the endless books, my attention would have rested with my curiosity to know who was speaking. So instead of trying to resist, I followed the voice.

As I looked down the corridor from where the voice came, the words remained a blurred sound. Standing at the corridor's entrance I gave Holy Spirit a curious look. As I stepped in and ventured down the short hall, the words coming from the man who spoke began to be more distinguishable. I began to notice that the words were unraveling a teaching. As clarity began permitting me to hear, even on my journey to find the man, his words were instantly beginning to open new realms of understanding to me. In fact, I had not met someone who taught like this man taught, other than Jesus, Holy Spirit or Wisdom. He was unfolding secrets that had been hidden ever since the foundations of Heaven and Earth were created.

Reaching the end of the corridor, I entered into a similar room to the room that I had just left; a room full of endless books and scrolls. To the right of me sat a man who appeared to be in his mid-seventies. On his wood crafted chair he sat dignified. The chair was not at all an ordinarily crafted chair. Its chiseled details were sculpted by skilled hands, immaculately made to seat one of importance. At the man's feet sat three men. The man on the left was in his early forties. The man in the middle was in his late fifties, and the man to the right was nearing 70 years of age.

The older gentleman who was seated on the chair concocted a teaching for these three that was intricate as well as broad. The man spun words as a master of eloquence. Standing at a distance I listened for a time taking in every word.

"Who are these men?" I eventually asked Holy Spirit.

"Those three men sitting on the floor are former pastors who each pastored churches of 400 people before they ascended to Heaven for eternity. The old man on the chair teaching them, before his ascension, was a former homeless man."

Shocked, I asked, "How is it that this man is able to teach so well, and to such an important audience?"

Holy Spirit answered bluntly, yet honestly. "It is because he was faithful with what was given to him, and they were not. So, therefore, he is considered to be in a higher place in Heaven than these three."

Holy Spirit went on to share, "Where these three men who are sitting on the floor were given 400 each to steward, this former homeless man was only given two friends. He loved those two friends deeply. He laid down his life for them over and over again. This is why he is considered to be in a higher place in Heaven."

Knowledge, Wisdom and Revelation

"Surely these men must have laid down their lives for the 400 who each of them were called to pastor," I said to Holy Spirit.

"To some extent they did, Nameless One," Holy Spirit responded. "But for a bulk of their ministries, they led for their own gain and for their own names to be great instead of out of a love for those they were called to shepherd. True leaders lead not to appease their insecurities; they lead because they love. Remember, everyone's heart will one day be tested. Listen to his story, Nameless One. It is a story that I hold close to my heart."

"When this man dwelled on Earth, he had special favour with a restaurant in a downtown area in the city where he lived. The manager would often leave food outside in the alleyway specifically for him to eat so that he would not starve. Every time this man would receive food from this restaurant, he would split his food in thirds for his two friends. They would all sit together on the street corner eating and enjoying one another's friendship. He was one who loved God with all of his heart. Double mindedness did not exist in him, and still does not. He lived a life fully devoted to loving God and loving others. He would counsel his two friends through their heartaches of losing their families. He was a true pastor to them. He was a true shepherd. He lived life alongside of them. He was by no means out of arms reach, but at hand. He was a father to these men."

"When the restaurant went out of business, the three had no more food. The men were nearing starvation. Their faces were hollowing. Their strength was leaving. One day, this man stumbled across a small sum of money that was laying on the ground. No one was around in sight of him to ask if someone had dropped it. Immediately he went into a store and bought his two street-adopted sons some food. The thought did not even cross his mind to buy food for himself. When he found his two friends, he fed them and enjoyed every moment watching their hunger being filled. This man died later that night from starvation. He was a martyr for love. He was a true ambassador of the gospel. Greater love has no one than this, than to lay down one's life for his friends."

I looked at the man with new reverence. Authority wielded his words as he continued teaching the former pastors about the love of God.

I continued listening when a sight of familiarity caught my eyes. In the distance with about 50 books stacked around him was the young apostolic boy who I had previously met in the Garden of Intimacy. I was surprised to see Wisdom standing next to him, teaching the boy.

Holy Spirit broke my attention, "I want you to see something, Nameless One."

Following Holy Spirit, I began straying from the teacher and his pupils, as well as Wisdom and the apostolic boy.

"Isn't Wisdom coming with us, Holy Spirit? Why is she staying with the apostolic boy?" I asked.

"She is not coming with us this time. Wisdom cannot follow us where we are going right now. For the time being she will be a teacher to the upcoming apostle. Even though Wisdom is a highly ranked angel, she is not permitted in the room where I am about to lead you. I am leading you to the Grand Room of this library. This is a room where only the Godhead and the sons and daughters of God have access."

As I walked away with Holy Spirit, I could still hear both Wisdom and the elderly teacher speaking words that I knew would ring throughout my spirit for quite some time.

Through many different corridors, twists and turns, Holy Spirit led me to the Grand Room of Heaven's library. And grand it was indeed. Standing just outside of it I could see that the bookshelves were endless. Looking forth I could see that the room seemingly had no end.

I was about to take a step into this section of the library when I felt Holy Spirit's hand press against my chest cautioning me. "Before you enter this room, there is a revelation that must be caught. In this room are some of Heaven's purest pearls of revelation. If you go in when you are not ready, you will risk trampling upon them."

"What revelation is it that I need to know before entering?" I asked.

Without answering my question, Holy Spirit walked over to a book shelf that was right outside the Grand Room. He pulled a book from one of the top shelves and handed it to me.

"Take a look at this book," He said to me.

Much like the John G. Lake book I read from the library, this one was unexpectedly heavy. The book's cover was light blue and had silver trim around its edging.

"This book is a record of revelation that rested upon Jack Frost's ministry. Jack was one of the pioneers for a revelation of the Father heart of God. This is the revelation you must receive before entering."

Looking at the book intrigued, I was about to open it, when Holy Spirit stopped me. "You may want to take a seat before opening that," Holy Spirit said while laughing lightly.

I went and sat down at one of the library's tables. Laying the book upon the wooden surface, I could feel the glory of God radiating from it. I opened the book, and was met by the anointing that rested on Jack Frost's ministry. Chills ran throughout my entire body. Emotion swept over me. A revelation of self-worth and acceptance did as well. I felt so loved in that moment. It was a familiar feeling that reminded me of when I first sat upon the sandy shore in Heaven. Looking into this book was like looking into the sunrise itself. False perceptions of who I thought I was were burning away, revealing who I truly was. I felt sure of my identity. Even though I had not yet met the Father, I was beginning to trust who Holy Spirit and Jesus said He was.

"This is the anointing that unlocks the brokenhearted into healing," Holy Spirit said. Yet when He spoke, I felt so moved that I could not even respond.

Holding me by the hand, Holy Spirit gently helped me to my feet and began to walk with me towards the Great Room. When I took my first step into the room, I felt an even deeper wave of emotion rise in me.

"This is one of the most important places in Heaven," Holy Spirit said, as though He were showing me something precious to His heart.

"These specific books that you see before you are the books of remembrance. They are books that contain every detail about every single son and daughter of God. Nothing was withheld from being written in these books except the sin of humankind. Every thought they have ever thought is recorded here. Every desire of their hearts are written in these books. Every laugh they have laughed is documented here as well as every tear they have cried. Not a single prayer or conversation with God or with another human was left out."

I was amazed at how much was recorded for each person. There was not just a single bookshelf for a single person. For each son and daughter, there were hundreds of bookshelves packed with books.

"Who is the author of all these books?" I asked Holy Spirit.

"The Father," He responded.

"The Father loves His children so much that He has sat down Himself and has written out every single detail about each. His love is never ending. His affection never ceasing."

The Father's love was so great. As glorious as all of Heaven was, I was deeply moved by the fact that it was the desires of God's children's hearts that were some of Heaven's most precious pearls.

"I feel that I am ready to meet Him Holy Spirit. I am ready to meet my Father. Please bring me to Him."

"Soon, Nameless One. There is one more place that I must show you. Then I will lead you to Him."

"Where is it that you need to take me?" I asked.

Holy Spirit responded like a friend speaking to a friend. "In your meeting with the Son of Man, He told you that you would see Him again at the Hall of Mantles. This is where I must lead you."

Mantling Generations

Corridor by corridor, Holy Spirit and I travelled through the library. We reached the library's end sooner than I assumed we would. However, we must have crossed through half a dozen grand rooms before reaching the door that led to the Hall of Mantles. As we came to the door, written above it in golden script read Psalm 22:18: *"They divide my garments among them."*

Stepping through the door, I immediately saw four children running down the Hall playing tag. The sight brought a smile to my face knowing that they could have so much fun in such a place of importance. The children's joy reminded me of how Holy Spirit seemed to view life.

Other than the four children, the Hall was empty. When I had imagined the Hall of Mantles prior to that moment, I had always pictured it being much more lively.

Recognizing my thoughts, Holy Spirit answered my question before I could voice it. "This is the south side of the Hall of Mantles, Nameless One. Once we reach the north side it will not seem seem as recluse."

We began walking north, yet it was not long until we reached a small room on the left hand side of the hallway. Holy Spirit walked right up to the door, opened it and motioned for me to step inside.

"Before we reach the north end of the Hall I have a special surprise waiting for you in here," Holy Spirit said.

Stepping in, I saw that the room was a small study. In the quiet room three men sat at a wooden desk. A bald man who was the shortest of the three, stood up from his chair. "Holy Spirit! Come in. Come in. It is wonderful to see you!" The other two stood up, welcoming Holy Spirit and me into the room.

Holy Spirit laughed His well-known laugh. "Hello all! I have been wanting the three of you to meet a friend of mine."

Holy Spirit looked over to me. "Nameless One, I want to introduce you to Elijah, Elisha, and Gehazi."

At the very mention of the three's names, shivers shot right through me. What an honour! I reached out to shake each of the men's hands. Each man shone in brilliant light. However Elijah was a radiant torch compared to the two others. Elijah was a surprisingly hairy man. He wore a simple girdle made of leather. His eyes had an intense gaze to them. They were the type of eyes that saw beyond the past and present, deep into the future. I knew that those eyes saw things that God only allows a select few to see. Only those who He calls His friends. However, even though there was an intensity to Elijah, there was also an undeniable depth of joy.

Elisha was the short, bald man who first welcomed us. He could only be described as jovial. Even when no one was talking, you could often hear him gently laughing.

Just as Elijah and Elisha, Gehazi shone in heavenly splendor, yet he looked the most normal out of the three in appearance. You could see that he had insight, as Elijah did and zeal as Elisha. Yet, Gehazi seemed to carry a much shallower grid for both. Still, it was undeniable that he held authoritative wisdom. It was wisdom that I desired to have deposited into me. Gehazi stood proud, honoured to be with Holy Spirit, Elijah, Elisha and me in the study.

"It is an honour to meet all of you," I said.

"The honour is all ours!" Elisha jumped in, not giving the others a chance to speak. I still found it fascinating to see how personalities shone so brightly in Heaven.

Elijah gave Elisha a knowing look and then spoke. "Those of us who have already ascended dream of having the privilege to encourage and speak into those who still walk the Earth. We hope that what we have to impart will help the King of kings to bring an awakening within the nations."

The only way to describe Elijah's voice was that it sounded godly. I had never met a man, other than a member of the Trinity whose voice was so profound that it sounded like rushing waters. His voice carried a similar tone to Holy Spirit's, because he was so refined and practiced in speaking the word of the Lord. All of us took a seat at the wooden table in the study's centre. After we were all settled, Elijah began unpacking the weighty introduction to their teaching:

"There is a revelation concerning mantles that is going to grip the church in this day. As individuals take up their mantles, it is necessary to understand the purpose of their mantles. A mantle is not something that should be used to build your name. If your name is found through your successes, then your life will be built upon what others say about you instead of who God says you are. God's people need to understand that they stand before Him before they stand before man. I have spoken to kings. I have counseled them. Yet they were my secondary audience. The one true God is my primary audience because everything we do is for His glory, not our own. No, a mantle is to make an impact beyond your inner self. It is to leave an influence even beyond your own generation. The effects of a well utilized mantle should turn history by causing a ripple effect throughout generations to come."

Elisha then cut in, "My teacher, Elijah, understood this better than most, you know. He never placed his identity in his calling. I still remember the day when he came to me. I was just plowing with the oxen, when Elijah came and threw his mantle onto me. When it fell onto me I felt the Lord's presence. I also felt very humbled that the Lord would call me. It was one of the most profound moments of my young life. Instead of hoarding his anointing, Elijah looked upon me and saw potential. He saw who I was truly created to be. And the act of him placing his mantle on me was his vow of commitment to fathering me into maturity. The younger generation needs fathers and mothers who are committed to sowing into their destinies."

"If your successes die with you, then you have missed the point of legacy entirely," Elijah said bluntly. "I meet many saints who have ascended here to Heaven. They have toiled their entire lives trying to build something for the kingdom, yet at their death, the world is often cut off from the great fruit of their lives. When I walked the earth, I pioneered a move of restoration in Israel between man and God. I did a great thing for God's advancement. Where I pioneered the move, I had risen up Elisha to take care of what I built. If I had not done this, the ground which I gained would have been reclaimed back because there was no one stationed at the breech. Even though I did great things, the fruit of my work lasting was dependent on my willingness to father and Elisha's willingness to be fathered by me. Raising up successors is tremendously important if you want to impact the generations. You may be able to sculpt a bow out of wood, but your children are the arrows. Without them, your work is just a monument frozen still on history's timeline. Your labour becomes stagnant instead of organic. It is often pride and ignorance that hinders people from letting their children stand on their shoulders to touch higher skies."

Elisha started speaking again, "I left everything to serve and follow Elijah. I made sure that there was nothing for me to come back to. My hunger to understand the ways of God drove me to never leave Elijah's side. And as a father, he allowed me to stay with him. The day that Elijah was taken to Heaven in a whirlwind was both one of the saddest moments, and one of the most profound in my life. My greatest friend was taken from me, yet I saw a man who loved the generations so much to the point where he gave a double portion of everything he achieved spiritually to me. At that point in my life it was the most selfless thing I had ever seen."

Elisha continued, "Even though I saw this great act, I failed where my father Elijah succeeded. Elijah allowed what he carried to be passed onto me, which permitted me to receive the double portion of his spirit. You have read about the anointing I carried. I walked in such an anointing that when I died, a man who was dead was thrown onto my corpse and the man shot right back to life again. Most see this as a great testimony about the anointing I carried. They see it as a triumph and as something to aspire to. But this was actually a testimony of how the anointing that I carried died with me, instead of being passed onto the next generation. I was unable to pass the torch that I carried to my servant Gehazi, which would have been my greatest feat for God's kingdom. In many ways, my anger towards Gehazi held me back from properly fathering him. There were times when he would do something foolish, and instead of walking along side of him to maturity as Elijah did with me, I allowed my anger to lead me instead of my desire for his success."

It was sobering for me to hear someone who I held in such high regard speaking of his failures so openly.

There was silence for a moment, when Holy Spirit spoke up, "Gehazi, do you have anything to share?"

Gehazi looked up modestly. "I do," he said. "I was Elisha's servant, just as Elisha was Elijah's. My story is short, yet it is a warning for the last day church. It is my privilege to share it. After Elijah ascended, Elisha tried to father me. He took me under his wing. I would see Elisha performing miracles that the great Elijah did. It was unquestionable that Elisha was blessed by his mentor, because he did even more miracles than even Elijah did. If Elisha received double of what Elijah carried, can you imagine what I was destined to walk in? I tried to perform the miracles that Elisha did, yet I could not because there was something in my heart preventing me from receiving as a son should. There was a part of me that could not receive what Elisha carried. Instead of doing what my father did, I just told stories about him in the king's court. This is my warning for the last day church. The last day church needs to walk in the spirit of sonship and daughtership, instead of the spirit of an orphan. Instead of just telling the stories of their forefathers as though their works were legendary, this generation needs to learn to take up where their fathers and mothers of the faith have left off. They need to make the legends their reality because a father's finish line is supposed to be a son's starting point. It was both Elisha's incapability to father well and my failure to receive as a son which stopped the anointing from being passed to me."

Holy Spirit was stone faced, which seemed out of character for Him. I could tell that this was something that He was very passionate about.

Elijah then spoke again, "The spirit of Elijah is resting upon the church. Its purpose is to turn the hearts of the fathers and mothers back to the children and the hearts of the children back to their fathers and mothers. Otherwise a curse will be released over the land. What is the curse you ask? It is more dreadful than you would think. The curse is fatherlessness and motherlessness. It takes both a father willing to give, and a son willing to receive, working together to bridge anointing through generations. God has not created man to be a one-hit-wonder. He has created man to leave a rich heritage and inheritance. I tell you the truth, one of the greatest threats to this generation of upcoming leaders is a worshipful heart towards their own callings. Really they need to walk in a heart such as Moses and David did. Moses longed to see the Promised Land, yet rejoiced when he knew that his spiritual son Joshua would lead Israel into the land instead of him. David longed to build God a temple, yet rejoiced in the fact that his son Solomon would do it instead. A father dreams of his son going further than he does."

Elijah, Elisha and Gehazi then did something that I did not expect. They all stood up from the wooden table and surrounded me. Each laid their right hand on the top of my head and began to bless me as though I were receiving and impartation on behalf of the whole church.

Gehazi began, "I bless this generation to succeed where I myself failed. I bless you to be able to receive what fathers and mothers in the faith have to offer. I bless you to be teachable and honorable. I declare over you eyes to see the glory that those who walk in maturity carry."

Elisha then spoke, "I bless this generation to see past themselves into the glory of upcoming children. I bless this generation to multiply what they carry through meekness and humility."

Elijah then finished off the prophetic declaration by saying, "I bless this generation to dream beyond themselves. I bless them to dream for their children and their children's children. Let unity pour like oil throughout history, blending anointings to create a new fragrance of legacy for the nations to experience. Let sonship and daughtership take shape within the heart of the Bride."

Holy Spirit then placed a hand on each of my shoulders and whispered softly into my right ear, "He who has ears let him hear what the Spirit says to the church."

Staying The Course

Holy Spirit led me down the Hall of Mantles farther north, away from the room where I met Elijah, Elisha and Gehazi. The Hall was not straight, but instead followed a steady curve to the right. After my meeting with the three prophetic leaders, I felt different. I felt as though I was carrying something new and of great significance.

This side of the Hall was still quiet, other than the sound of children playing. However, as we travelled north, a fresh sound began to stir. Instead of remaining on its steady curve, the Hall began straightening. The more we walked on, the more the sound's volume increased. It was the sound of a multitude of people.

As each step passed, the Hall began to take on a more elegant and royal expression. I then saw in the distance a multitude of people, many of which I had first seen in the Garden of Intimacy. As I strolled down the stony hallway, I ran my hand over the sacred inscriptions that were engraved into the walls. Where inscriptions were absent, mantles hung as monuments.

Holy Spirit held out a hand pointing at the mantles, "Every single mantle that has ever been worn by a child of God is displayed here as a monument. Each is a reminder and testimony to what God has done in and through each person who wore it. Some of these mantles were only worn by one person, where others that were utilized well have been worn by many."

Each mantle stood proud, projecting different mandates and callings. The mantles were many different colours. Some were red, others blue or yellow. Every colour and shade was represented. Some mantles were colours that I had never seen before; where others were cloaks of many colours. Some were simple and others were majestic, ornamented with gems and gold. There were also a few mantles made of fir and others that almost looked like armor. There were prophet mantles, apostle mantles, business mantles, mantles for mothering and fathering, you name it.

"This is the Hall of Mantles, Nameless One. It is the place where the Son of Man distributes mantles to each saint."

"Holy Spirit, why are there so many of the saints here who were in the Garden?" I asked.

Responding He said, "Look to the end of the Hall."

I looked over thousands of saints who were standing in a single line, and saw a brilliant sight at the Hall's end. Jesus was there. One by one, saints would walk up to the Son of Man to stand before Him. Jesus would then pull a mantle off of Himself and place it on whoever was standing before Him. To some, He would only give one mantle. To others He bestowed many. The most I watched Him place upon one person was 12. He wore every mantle Himself and was distributing them as He saw fit. Not a single mantle was the same as another. Every saint who received bore fresh zeal in their eyes because with each mantle came an increased sense of purpose and mandate.

Staying The Course

"Now that you have received an impartation to understand the mantling of generations, you will know how to steward a mantle properly. Remember what Elijah told you."

Holy Spirit then began quoting something that Elijah had said to me, "'A mantle is not something that should be used to build your name. If your name is found through your successes, then your life will be built upon what others say about you instead of who God says you are. The effects of a well utilized mantle should turn history by causing a ripple effect throughout generations to come.'"

I stepped into the lineup that consisted of thousands of people. I was incredibly eager to meet with Jesus again face to face. As I stood in the line, I watched the others intently, when all of a sudden something happened that caught me off guard. Many of the saints would begin with their full attention on Jesus, but then would start getting distracted by the different mantles that hung on the walls. They would begin wandering from the line to stand before the mantles that drew their attention. They would stand there staring, eyes agape.

Holy Spirit began unpacking what was happening. "The men and women who are straying from this line are the ones who have decided to give up in their seasons of training. Only through proper training, led by me, can someone properly carry their mantle or mantles with integrity. Unfortunately, many stop halfway through the valley before they get to the mountaintop. These men and women became distracted and took their eyes off of the Son, which made them weary and unable to continue. He is the source of rest. Now, these men and women are coveting the mantles and works of others."

I looked again at the mantles that hung upon the ancient walls. Many great men and women's mantles were there that I could see. I could see Moses' mantle that had the appearance of a simple beige cloak, which marked a noble and humble leader. I saw Peter's mantle which shone in solid bronze. His mantle looked more like armor than it did a cloak. Many of the wandering saints stood in front of a single mantle, which was a deep royal red cloak. On the cloak's front was an enormous red and yellow gem stone right in the centre of it to hold the two ends together. I knew in my spirit that this was Paul the apostle's mantle.

The saints would stare at the mantles in a state of mourning, believing in their hearts that they could never achieve the same feats that these men and women did. This left them still and stagnant.

By the time all of this had happened, hundreds in the line in front of me had already been mantled. It seemed as though time was greatly sped up. Then the oddest thing began to take place. Some of the saints who left the line actually began reaching up and grabbing at the different mantles from the walls. I saw many saints trying to place these mantles that were not their own upon themselves. One man grabbed one of the larger mantles, which looked like a breastplate of white gold with a large sapphire stone in the centre of it. Placing the mantle on himself, a satisfied smile spread across his face. However, when he tried to walk, the mantle that he carried was too heavy for him to carry. He could not even take a single step. I then watched as a woman grabbed a smaller, and much more delicate mantle, made from silk. She tried to stretch the mantle over herself, but it was too small.

Holy Spirit cut in, "It is such a shame. Those who are not confident enough in their sonship and daughtership have great trouble understanding that the Godhead has woven a specific and special mantle for every single person. By coveting a mantle that was designed for someone else, they are indeed discrediting their own uniqueness. There are times when someone does inherit a mantle from other eras of history, but these are to never be self-appointed; they are only appointed by the Godhead."

Holy Spirit pointed to the man who was attempting to wear the white gold breastplate. "That mantle there was originally worn by a great evangelist who brought the gospel to many remote areas throughout the nations. He was known to much of the world after his death and is still remembered and revered by the church. The man trying to wear the mantle actually has the call to start a small business. Many in his community will be saved, healed and delivered if he chooses to take up his true mantle. Often people will place their self-worth in their achievements. If in their own eyes the desire of their hearts or the call over their lives seems insignificant, they will idolize a call that they feel is greater than their own. However, every calling and heart desire is significant and important to the Father."

Holy Spirit then pointed to the woman who tried putting on the silk mantle. "That woman there has the call of an apostle over her life. She is called to plant churches throughout the nations and to create an apostolic network that will stretch across different places in the world. Yet because of discrimination she has experienced in the past, she struggles with a lack of confidence that is preventing her from picking up her true apostolic mantle. She is now trying to squeeze into a smaller mantle due to her insecurities."

"What happens if they never change the way that they think about themselves and refuse to pick up their ordained mantle?" I asked.

Holy Spirit responded, "Then that mantle and mandate will be given to someone else, either in this generation or in a generation to come. The word of God will never turn back void. When you watched Jesus place numerous mantles on one person, some were mantles that were originally someone else's to wear. Since they rejected their calling, the Son of Man gave it to someone else who has already proven that they have been faithful with what was given to them. Many people will come to this Hall numerous times in their lifetime to take on different mandates and anointings when the Son of Man calls them."

Once Holy Spirit was finished clarifying what had taken place, thousands in the line in front of me had already been mantled by the Son of Man. Now only four stood in the line between Jesus and me. As Jesus mantled the first in the line, I tried to overhear what He was speaking to the man. Yet I did not hear a sound. It was interesting, I could watch Jesus place mantles on the man, and even discern what the mantles were for, but I could not hear what He said to him. What Jesus said to him was for his ears alone. The same happened for the second, third and fourth before me. Each was mantled by Jesus and sat under words from Him that no one could hear but them.

Then came my turn. I stood before the Son of Man yet again. Face to face.

Equipped With Forgotten Tools

As Holy Spirit stood by my side, Jesus waited wonderfully before me. Stepping forward, He gave me a hug and a kiss on my cheek.

"It's good to see you again," He said to me as He held both of my shoulders with His gentle hands. I do not know how I didn't realize this before, but Jesus bore the same green and orange eyes that Holy Spirit had. Those deep eyes burned like a passionate bonfire of love.

As I looked at Jesus, I could see that He wore every mantle that existed. Any type of mantle you could think of or imagine was upon the Son of Man. He wore each with flawless integrity and wisdom.

"There was a time before I was crucified when men divided my garments amongst themselves. Now I hand them out myself freely. Are you ready to receive your mantles?" Jesus asked me.

"Of course, my Lord," I said confidently.

Jesus then looked at me the way a teacher would look at His student. It was not a look that was intimidating; it was a look that filled me with courage. Jesus was looking into me. He was looking into my potential and I could feel confidence in who I was in Him stirring inside of me like a fire being stoked.

The Son of Man then said, "Many people live their lives casting the responsibility of the Kingdom aside, yet everyone who has professed me as Lord has a mandate. Once someone receives a new mantle, it is a declaration that they will step into new realms of influence. In new realms of influence there is heightened responsibility. To those who receive a mantle, each will be held accountable to what was given. To whom much is given, much is required."

Everything in me wanted to receive whatever the Lord had for me, no matter the cost. I postured my heart to receive.

Discerning my heart posture, Jesus then began pulling mantles off of himself and placing them upon me. The moment each mantle would touch me I could feel a grace of anointing being released over my life. As He would place each mantle upon me, He would then explain the purpose and function of each mantle. In that moment, He placed a total of seven mantles upon me.

"I have not only summoned you here to mantle you," Jesus said. "I brought you here that you might be fully equipped for the battle that is set before you."

Jesus then began checking the armor that adorned me. He straightened my crown, which was my helmet of salvation. He tightened my breastplate of righteousness, retied my shoes of the preparation of the gospel of peace, and made sure that the belt of truth around my waist was secure. Jesus then began polishing my shield of faith and my double handed broad sword, which was the word of God.

Equipped With Forgotten Tools

As Jesus secured and polished my armor and weapons, I was very moved that the greatest man who had ever lived served so well. I felt the same emotion that I assume the disciples must have felt when Jesus washed their feet. The emotion that I experienced was an overwhelming sense of wonder. Wonder as to how someone so great, powerful and awe-inspiring was at the same time so meek and lowly. I had never in the whole of my life heard of a general who not only led His army, but also geared them for battle.

"You look good," the Son of Man said lightheartedly. He then remarked more seriously, "You are not fully armed for battle yet, though. There are different tools that I am releasing to the church in this day for the purpose of healing the nations. These are weapons that have been long forgotten, yet will soon be remembered. Never forget this though, friend; what I give you are tools, not toys. They are to be wielded with the greatest of integrity. If only zeal wields these tools then great harm will be done. Yet if only wisdom wields, then these gifts will not be used to their greatest capacity. Both wisdom and zeal must wield these weapons. Both counsel and might."

Jesus held my gaze for what felt like a drawn-out moment, then reached into His robe and grabbed an object. The Son of Man then handed to me the first of these forgotten tools. This first weapon was a mighty war hammer. The head of this hammer was about the size of a grown man's forearm. The hammer's shaft was about three and a half feet long. Across the hammer on both its shaft and head were hundreds of gem stones crafted right into its metal. As I held the hammer in my right hand, it rested in my palm heavily. Since the hammer's weight was so significant, I knew that I could never wield this hammer in my own strength, only in God's. As I looked at the finely ornamented hammer, I saw that chiseled into the war hammer's head was Jeremiah 23:29, which says, "'Is not my word like a fire?' Says the LORD, 'And like a hammer that breaks the rock in pieces?'"

Jesus then spoke, bringing clarity to the hammer's purpose. "This hammer is the anointing to cause an instant shift in the atmosphere over entire regions through prophetic declaration. With one swing of this hammer, an entire nation can experience breakthrough. Is not my word like a fire? And like a hammer that breaks the rock in pieces? This hammer's strike can break the stone hearts of the masses, so that they can become hearts of flesh that are penetrable to me."

Jesus then handed me the second tool. In my left hand the Son of Man placed another hammer. Yet this one was much smaller for intricate working. This hammer was very light and its head was not larger than a man's hand. This hammer also looked much more normal than the hammer that I held in my right hand. The hammer was made from an extremely hard medal, yet was not flashy in appearance compared to its counterpart. Across this hammer's head was written 1 Corinthians 3:11, which says, "For no other foundation can anyone lay than that which is laid, which is Jesus Christ."

"This hammer is to build new foundations and to fix old foundations that have become cracked," Jesus said. "In this day, there will be a quickening in apostolic and prophetic working, both to build and for reformation. The true apostolic and prophetic ministries are being restored. A wisdom in how to build according to the Spirit of God is being released."

Jesus then pulled something off of Himself that hung around His neck and placed it around my own. It was a key that hung from a chain. As I rolled the key in between a finger and my thumb I noticed that written on this key was Isaiah 22:22, which says; "The key of the house of David I will lay on his shoulder; So he shall open, and no one shall shut; And he shall shut, and no one shall open."

The Son of Man spoke reverently, "This is the third tool. It is the key of David that is written of in Revelation 3:7. In this season I am training my Bride how to wield it with me. She will open doors for the Kingdom of Heaven which no man can close, and close doors for the kingdom of darkness that no man can open. Only those who understand how to carry David's strongest attribute will walk in the authority to wield this key. They must learn to be men and women after my own heart. They must learn to allow their deep to call out to my deep."

As I still was rolling the ancient key between my fingers Jesus handed me the final tool. He gave me an iron scepter, which He strapped onto my back. The scepter had a daunting look to it. Every time I looked upon it, I would almost forget to breathe. It was not that the scepter was incredibly beautiful; in fact, it looked quite plain. It was that this scepter carried undeniable authority. It carried an authority that only kings and queens could exercise.

On the scepter was written Revelation 2:26-27, which reads, "And he who overcomes, and keeps my works until the end, to him I will give power over the nations 'He shall rule them with a rod of iron; They shall be dashed to pieces like the potter's vessels' as I also have received from my Father.'"

"This scepter is the authority to rule over the nations with me," Jesus remarked. "Often when men or women go into remote areas to preach the kingdom, they go in believing that they are entering into someone else's territory. Really, they have inherited the nations with me from the Father. Wherever you tread your foot is land that you have inherited because of your royal rebirth. There is a great identity shift taking place within the sons and daughters of God. Holy Spirit is to teach orphans that they are sons and daughters, then to teach sons and daughters that they are fathers and mothers. Lastly, He is to show fathers and mothers that they are kings and queens. Holy Spirit is training the church to not only worship at my feet, but also to stand up and to take a seat on my throne with me. This is the age where kings and queens will be trained to reign with me."

I could feel a sense of purpose rising inside of me. I could feel it rising on behalf of the entire Bride of Christ. In that moment I knew that the church was going to step out from the corner of the field onto the centre stage of the world. With both counsel and might wielding these tools, entire regions would be transformed into the very likeness of Heaven.

Jesus grabbed my shoulders again and spoke affectionately to me. "Remember, Nameless One, you need to walk through the garden of intimacy to get to the Tree of Life, which carries the leaves that bring healing to the nations."

When Jesus called me 'Nameless One' I looked away in thought. *If I never truly know who I am, everything that I have received here will be for nothing.*

My eyes sprung up to Jesus, and just as I was about to ask Him a question I saw an unexpected sight. In Jesus' hands He held several different golden leaves from the Tree of Life. He began pinning them on my breastplate. "It is now time for you to meet our Father. When you do, you will never be the same again. You will never be nameless again."

I looked over to Holy Spirit and was met by His proud eyes. Jesus then pulled me close to Him, embracing me in a hug. "Close your eyes," He said. As soon as my eyes shut, I was lost in intimacy.

Jesus whispered into my ear, "When you have seen me, you have seen the Father. For no one comes to the Father except through me."

Journeying Through An Endless Ocean

When I opened my eyes I was back where my adventure began. Upon Heaven's shore I gazed on the sunrise, which still effortlessly stole my breath. When I first came to this wonderful place the ocean roared in chaos. In many ways it reflected my tormented consciousness. A consciousness that was unsure and confused. Now the ocean rested peacefully, without ripple, as still as a lake.

To my left sat Holy Spirit, and to my right sat my friend, Jesus. Being with them, I felt completely at peace.

"Are you excited to meet our Father?" Jesus asked.

"I am very excited; however, the journey to get to this point is one that I would not give away for anything in the world."

A Timeless Journey

Holy Spirit gazed into the sunrise. He spoke to me without even turning His head. "You should know that meeting Him is no mere destination. Some consider marriage a destination. Others consider landing their dream job a destination. To some death is a form of ending. Yet when they arrive to each there are only more questions. When you know God as your eternal friend, there are no endings and no destinations; there are only new beginnings."

Holy Spirit gazed into my eyes with those same green and orange orbs that burned into me the first day I met Him. He then spoke words that ignited a new fire within me. "Meeting the Father is no destination," He said. "In fact, once you meet Him, you will begin the wildest adventure you have ever lived."

I sat soaking under Holy Spirit's words. And as I sat I waited. I waited because I knew in my spirit that something was about to happen that would bring me closer to the Father. And something did. It was something hardly subtle, yet it was gentle and beautiful. Looking into the eye of the golden sun, I saw white rose pedals begin to rain from the sky. They gracefully danced down the soft trails that the breeze had paved for them, and rested upon the steadied ocean. One by one, the elegant pedals kissed the water. As they fell, I could not help but laugh at the sheer beauty of the scene unfolding before my eyes. At the sound of my laughter, Jesus and Holy Spirit began to laugh with me. We laughed together as eternal friends would. We were undignified in our joy. Not a hint of hiddenness existed between the three of us in that moment. I was fully exposed to them, and them to me. Innumerable pedals descended until the entire ocean was covered. The only part that remained bare was a straight pathway of ocean floor about six feet wide, leading into the far unknown.

The three of us stood up on the sandy beach. Jesus and Holy Spirit waited for me to welcome the new path set before me. I knew that when I began to walk this watery road, I would never be the same again. I stood before the ocean trail, allowing a stirring for adventure and freedom to push my feet to walking. When I placed my left foot on the watery ground, it did not sink. As I lifted my right foot to take another step, I found that my whole body was supported upon the solid road. I looked back at my two friends. Behind them was the emerald forest that I had seen earlier, and beyond the forest were the many mountains made from various gems. What a wonderful place, I thought again. Holy Spirit and Jesus both laughed and motioned for me to start walking.

With the ocean beneath me and floating white rose pedals on on either side of me, I walked on water. It was a timeless journey across a sea of glass, and into the sunrise's steady embrace. The sun's touch on my face was a gift of promise. I was on my way to find Him whom my heart desired. I closed my eyes, taking in the perfume of endless rose pedals. The fragrance of intimacy and romance.

As I continued to walk forward, all scenery around me began to change. The changes were so subtle and perfect that I hardly perceived them.

At the end of the pathway along the sea of glass, I found myself standing in a throne room. I had read time and time again in the scriptures about different people experiencing the throne room in Heaven, but to experience it for myself was something new entirely. Beside the throne stood four mighty cherubim. Above it flew six elegant seraphim. However, I could not bring myself to give them even the slightest bit of attention. As magnificent as the angels were and as luxurious as the room was, I was unable to take my eyes off of the one who sat upon the throne. He was my heart's desire.

A Timeless Journey

The Father sat as a true Father should. He was fully inviting, not intimidating by the slightest of standards. His eyes never strayed from me. He just gazed, and smiled over me. Looking deep into His eyes I became lost. His eyes were an endless ocean of love through which I could swim forever.

I walked up to Him boldly. Confidently.

Some would assume that I would have bowed down and worshipped Him as He sat upon His throne. Yet this is not what I did at all. As the child that I am, I climbed up onto His lap. I laid my head against His mighty chest and listened to His love-filled heartbeat. His arms then wrapped around me, embracing me. He was the most comfortable place.

Without even thinking, words fell out from my lips. Even though my voice was faint, no more than a whisper, the Father heard me clearly.

"Who am I?" I asked.

The Father then began to speak. The words that emanated from Him were swords of light, so tangible that they pierced through any worries of rejection and shone throughout the caverns of my once darkened soul. Now there was no darkness. There were no fears or worries.

"That, young one, is one of the most profound questions that anyone could ever seek an answer to." The Father declared, "You have come for a name. You have come for an identity. You have come to know who you are. Since you have chosen to come to me for this, you will never be nameless again."

The Father then began to sing over me. It was not an elaborate song. In fact it was rather simple. However, its depth was by no means shallow. The Father sang over me a song of identity. His voice was as soft as a soothing cello, yet as strong as a mountain's roar. His voice both cradled me as a mother would, and poured strength into me like a loving father. And so, His song went like this:

> "My child, your name is *Accepted*."
> "I name you Significant. I name you Special."
>
> "Your name is *Precious* and *Priceless*. I name you *Important* and *Irreplaceable*."
>
> "Your name is *Beautiful*. Your name is *Brilliant*. You will now be known as *Beloved Child*."
>
> "You are not alone. You are wanted. You belong. You are loved. You are the apple of my eye and the greatest desire of my heart."
>
> "Your name is *Wielder of Light* and *Healer of Nations*. I name you *Creator of History* and *Ambassador of Heaven*."
>
> "You are my child, and you shall be so forevermore."

As the Father sang, life locked the door in my heart so that a crisis in my identity could not have reign within me. My heart was no longer callused stone, it was refined to the most precious of gold. I loved the Father wholeheartedly. And in that moment I loved myself wholeheartedly. I was His beloved child. On His lap. In His embrace, I would enjoy Him forevermore. I listened intently to His pounding heart. His heart that pounded for me. The heart of One who gave me not only one name, but many. He gave me my identity. I knew in that moment that for the rest of eternity, I would be on a timeless journey deeper into the heart of Him who my heart loves.

This is life. This is home.

Made in the USA
Charleston, SC
23 September 2014